THE MYSTERIES OF THE ANDES

Deep within the Andes Mountains of Peru lies a historical treasure beyond wildest dreams. It is the vast array of intricately etched stones—stones that show men coexisting with dinosaurs, stones that disrupt all versions of Genesis—that are the ultimate key to unlocking the secrets of Atlantis, the Deluge, UFOs, the history of mankind, and perhaps, the universe itself!

From his first stunned encounter with this stone bible in the secret museum of Dr. Cabrera in Ica, Peru, Charroux relates the startling evidence of our "primohistory"—of Earth visited throughout the ages by superintelligent life, of a superior civilization that vanished, but left a testimony to survive the perils of time!

❖

THE MYSTERIES OF THE ANDES is one in a series of Avon Books dedicated to exploring the lost secrets of ancient peoples and earlier times . . . secrets which challenge mankind today—and which may hold the key to our own future.

Other Avon Books in the series

THE MYSTERIES OF THE ANDES

BY ROBERT CHARROUX

Translated by Lowell Bair

AVON
PUBLISHERS OF BARD, CAMELOT AND DISCUS BOOKS

AVON BOOKS
A division of
The Hearst Corporation
959 Eighth Avenue
New York, New York 10019

© 1974 Editions Robert Laffont, S.A.
English translation copyright © 1977 by Avon Books
Published by arrangement with Editions Robert Laffont, S.A.
Library of Congress Catalog Card Number: 77-82252
ISBN: 0-380-01702-4

First Avon Printing, September, 1977

AVON TRADEMARK REG. U.S. PAT. OFF. AND IN
OTHER COUNTRIES, MARCA REGISTRADA,
HECHO EN U.S.A.

Printed in the U.S.A.

Contents

CONTENTS

What comes afterward is like what goes before.
What we can understand is insipid and sacrilegious.

It is maverick archaeologists, and adventurous ideas denigrated by official pundits, that acquaint the general public with prehistory and open doors to the unknown ancient world.

Preface

MAN IS COLD TO TRUTH and warm to falsehood, said La Fontaine.

We must, of course, be wary of what is called—often lightly—truth or self-evidence, especially where philosophy, religion or deep-seated belief is concerned. Falsehood is not inherently detestable and evil; if it were, we would have to banish poets and novelists, relinquish daydreams and, with dismay in our hearts, confront a life no longer made as pleasant as possible by errors and imagination.

The fact is that man has the fortunate privilege of being unable to distinguish falsehood from truth, and wiser men than I have never believed in either, but rather in a reflection, perceptible only to the mind, which Buddha called *maya,* illusion.

Yet, on the level of human activities and relations, it has been necessary to invent meanings for words intended to convey a judgment, and to give the name of truth to what should be regarded as genuine according to our senses and intellect.

It is within this frame of reference that I have always affirmed the authenticity of Glozel, and that I now affirm that the discovery of the Primohistoric Library of Ica is real, that the photographs published in this book were taken in Dr. Cabrera's sanctuary on the Plaza de Armas in Ica, and that thousands of the stones exist, with very old engravings on them that have already been examined by dozens of witnesses. Those stones will be presented to the public as soon as an agreement has been signed between Dr. Cabrera and the Peruvian government.

I question the honesty of anyone who expresses doubt about the existence or antiquity of those engraved stones. They revolutionize the study of human history and show that the prehistory taught in our time is full of errors and implausibilities.

But I do not expect the Conspiracy to admit it has been wrong; I expect it to reject the new vision of the past that I am proposing, a vision based not on hazardous speculation, but on palpable evidence thousands of years old. If that happens, readers of this book will be in a position to make an informed judgment.

R. C.

CHAPTER 1

Dr. Cabrera's Secret

HALF A CENTURY AGO, Colonel James Churchward stated that while he was serving with the British Army in India he had gone to a temple where he saw Naacal tablets revealing the mystery of creation and the history of human civilizations going back two hundred thousand years. Unfortunately he never gave the location of the temple or photographed any of the tablets, and so his story had to be taken entirely at face value. Archaeologists therefore rejected it, and they cannot be blamed for their disbelief, even if Churchward was sincere, which is a possibility that cannot be ruled out.

I have made an analogous discovery: eleven thousand engraved stones, stored in the secret museum of a surgeon in Ica, Peru, which relate the history of the world from sixty million years ago.

By means of precise, detailed images, these stones portray, without the shadow of a dubious interpretation, the life of dinosaurs in the Mesozoic era, and of a human race highly advanced in surgery, medicine, geography, technology and most of the sciences that we study today.

But, unlike Churchward, I have said where those extraordinary documents are and, with their owner's permission, anyone can see, touch and examine them. In short, I offer *proof* that my discovery is genuine.

A THUNDERCLAP IN PERU

Imagine Howard Carter, Lord Carnarvon and Callender entering the tomb of Tutankhamen and you will have some idea of the adventure I experienced at the end of April 1973 in Peru, between the Pacific and the Andes. I entered a sanctuary containing wonders incomparably older than the chariots, sarcophagi and amulets of the Theban Second Empire, and incomparably richer in teachings.

When they discovered the prehistoric library in the La Marche cave at Lussac-les-Châteaux, France, Léon Péricard and Stéphane Lwoff must have known that same ineffable exhilaration that makes one feel one could walk on water, fly through the air or pass through thick walls. It came over me when I first saw the vast array of stone books that had been patiently accumulated by their discoverer, Dr. Javier Cabrera Darquea, in his secret museum in Ica.

It was five o'clock in the afternoon of April 29, 1973, a date that will always stand out in my memories of my expeditions throughout the world. My wife and I had just traveled more than twelve thousand miles to explore places that haunted our imagination: Easter Island, with its six hundred giant statues; Tahiti; Huahiné, whose *maraes* are the ancestors of the Easter Island statues. But what was waiting for us in Ica far outshone the splendor of the monoliths of Hangaroa or the gray stone entablatures of Tahiti.

We were the first people from the Old World to see the thousands of engraved stones dating from ten, fifty or a hundred thousand years ago, or even sixty million years ago, according to Dr. Cabrera.

A stroke of luck that strongly resembled a miracle put us on the wondrous path while we were in the Nascan Desert. We had gone there to survey the *pistas* and drawings that I will discuss later in this book. My wife Yvette was looking for *huacos,* pieces of ancient painted pottery that are strewn over some areas of the pampa, near the famous drawings. It was April 27 and she intended to give them to me for my name day, two days later. As it turned out, I was to have an even better present than pottery fragments painted by the ancient Incas.

With our guide Edmond Wertenschlag of Lima, our Incan driver Emilio and the obliging agricultural engineer Alain Elias of Ica, we were trying to identify a huge drawing of a bird when Alain Elias opened the door to a forbidden world. To me, it was like a thunderclap of the Apocalypse.

DR. CABRERA'S COLLECTION

"In Ica," Alain Elias said to me, "there's an amazing man you ought to meet. He has a museum of engraved stones that's the only one of its kind."

"Stones with signs engraved on them?"

"No, the engravings show animals, people and scenes from everyday life going back to incredibly ancient times—to the Mesozoic or Tertiary era, if I'm not mistaken!"

"Scientists say there were no human beings in the Mesozoic, but it's possible that they're mistaken."

"Precisely, Señor Charroux. You're the one who can best understand Dr. Cabrera. He's read your books and he'll be glad to see you. Here's his address. . . . His secret museum is on the Plaza de Armas. Go to see him, but I must tell you beforehand that prehistorians have claimed his collection isn't genuine."

"Of course! If Dr. Cabrera has found some really valuable engraved stones, official archaeologists are sure to call them counterfeit, to cover up the inadequacy of their own research. It's standard procedure with them. What you've said makes me eager to see Dr. Cabrera's museum."

Alain Elias bent down, picked up a fragment of Nasca pottery and murmured as though to himself, "If the engravings are genuine, as I believe they are, all our ideas about the history of the world will have to be completely transformed. But scientists will never accept such a revolution."

His remark made a deep impression on me, as if it had been spoken in a tone of prophecy. I was probably influenced at that moment by the sight that lay before me: the arid desert was glittering as if it were covered with millions of precious stones and, in the direction of the Rio Grande, the sunlight was reflecting golden *pistas* on the clouds that merged into the mountains of the Pampa Colorada.

We continued our survey the next day, Saturday, and our trip to Ica was greatly slowed down by the Pan-American car race that took place on Sunday. Since the road was closed till two o'clock in the afternoon, we did not reach Ica till late in the evening.

A WORLD OF INTELLIGENT STONES

"Are you really the writer Robert Charroux?" Dr. Cabrera asked me.

"Yes, I am. This is my wife Yvette, who goes with me on all my expeditions, and this is our guide and interpreter, Edmond Wertenschlag of Lima."

The doctor embraced us warmly and took us into his museum.

It occupies the ground floor of a large building on

the Plaza de Armas in Ica, and is composed of five main rooms where he has gathered a prodigious collection of rounded or flat stones and blocks of andesite. (*See Figure 1*.) They are nearly all black or gray, though some pieces of eruptive rock have a lighter color and finer grain.

These stones, some of them weighing more than four hundred pounds, were entirely covered with engravings, so that they had to be turned over, which was sometimes difficult, in order to see the whole picture on them. Thousands of them had been placed on strong shelves; others, the heavier ones, rested close together on the floor, with a winding path among them so that they could be examined separately.

Nowhere else in the world, from India to Easter Island, from France to the sources of the Nile, had I ever seen such a collection of carved stones. They covered the walls and floors in bewildering profusion. I later learned that they were all classified and systematically arranged, but only Dr. Cabrera's practiced eyes and mind could discern the order in that seeming chaos.

Unprepared for such a sight, I found it awesome, marvelous. I stood speechless with amazement, lost in a mineral world that radiated an intelligence that had to be perceived mainly by the subconscious.

Dr. Cabrera must have enjoyed my astonishment for a few moments later he began guiding me through the museum and giving me explanations that my disconcerted mind did its best to register.

ARCHIVES WRITTEN BEFORE THE DELUGE

Dr. Javier Cabrera Darquea is a surgeon, a professor at the University of Ica, a physician at the workers' hospital of Ica, a member of the Regional Council of Ica, and a corresponding member of the International College of Surgery, besides being a prehistorian, an anthropologist and a biologist. A dark-haired elegant man in his early fifties, he is of average height and has a high forehead and eyes that sparkle with intelligence. He looks like his ancestor, Don Jeronimo Luis, who founded the city of Ica in 1563. Like him, he is a conquistador, but in the twentieth century: his conquests take place in the realm of science, and particularly prehistory. But while Don Jeronimo only founded a city, Dr. Cabrera may very well found an empire that will perpetuate his name till the end of the human world: after Herodotus, Plato, Buffon and Boucher de Perthes, he has brought to prehistory and the study of ancient civilizations a light that disturbs the obsolete views that are now taught in universities.

"My stones," he said to me, "come from the civilization of the first cultivated people on our planet. For an unknown reason, perhaps a natural cataclysm, that civilization disappeared, but the people of ancient Ica wanted to leave a testimony to it that would survive the perils of time. These archives came either directly from them, or from a more recent people who inherited the knowledge of their great ancestors.

"We can logically assume that those Superior Ancestors were Atlanteans who survived the destruction of their continent, settled in the region of Ica and left behind the talking stones of my collection.

"The first appearance of *Homo sapiens* has been dated at two or three million years ago, but that's a mistake. Man is much older than he's usually said to be. He coexisted with the dinosaurs that ruled the animal kingdom during the Mesozoic era.

"Those dinosaurs that lived at the end of the Mesozoic—the plesiosaurus, the diplodocus, the iguanodon and so on—survived into the Tertiary until a time when human beings knew them and struggled against them for supremacy.*

---

* On February 9, 1856, the *Illustrated London News* reported a strange discovery that had just been made in France. Workers digging a railroad tunnel between Saint-Dizier and Nancy found what they thought to be a giant black bat with a ten-foot wingspan. It uttered

"I began collecting my stones in 1966, but the first ones were found in 1961 by men searching for ancient pottery."

THE PRIMOHISTORIC LIBRARY OF ICA

The stone books of Ica reveal, sometimes clearly (it is enough to read the drawings), sometimes more obscurely (one must interpret), what the Atlanteans or the Unknown Ancestors knew about biology, natural history, surgery, geography, sociology, paleontology and most of the other scientific disciplines. It may be, in fact, that the whole history of the earth and the universe is related in drawings whose symbolism eludes the uninformed mind.

"We may be at the end of our time," said Dr. Cabrera. "That is, we may be about to experience a great cataclysm that clear-sighted people are beginning to foresee. The Americans have already buried a 'time capsule' containing the essentials of our civilization.

"The same thing must have happened in the very remote past. Man can't bequeath his knowledge to his children, but one human race can bequeath its knowledge to another. Knowledge has always been transmitted that way. You can judge for yourself, from the history of the world's peoples and what you'll see here."

Guiding us through the rooms of his museum, along the labyrinthine paths among the stones, he gave us a glimpse of the contents of the Primohistoric Library of Ica. We saw a succession of scenes that took place millions of years ago. In a setting of prehistoric plant

---

loud cries and died. A local scientist identified it as a pterodactyl, a flying reptile believed to have been extinct. The rocks in which the animal was discovered were more than a million years old. A hollow in them corresponded exactly to the shape of its body. The story was reprinted by the magazine *Fate* in May 1964.

It may have been a case of extraordinarily long hibernation by an animal that was nourished by the mother-water of the rocks.

life, vanished animals now studied by paleontologists were depicted in precise detail: brachiosaurs, tylosaurs, tyrannosaurs, brontosaurs, stegosaurs. (My lack of familiarity with such extinct species will explain any errors I may have made in this list.)

Men hunting dinosaurs are also shown. One of them, probably on his way back from fishing, since he carries a load of fish on his back, is attacking a dinosaur with arrows.

It is disconcerting to note that some drawings, apparently as old as the ones showing dinosaurs, depict animal species that, according to official science, appeared much later: ostriches, kangaroos, penguins, herons, bats, camels.

PREHISTORIANS PASS JUDGMENT

Dr. Cabrera is also surprised by this contemporaneity of animals that supposedly lived far apart in time, but the engravings on his stones ignore current scientific theory on that subject, and no doubt they are right. It is up to specialists to decide the matter if they can.

I will point out, with all due humility, that the sauropod, which lived during the Cretaceous period, in the time of the tyrannosaur, strangely resembled the kangaroo, through Ruth Moore has said that it might be called an "ostrich reptile." And there are pre-Columbian drawings that show a paleothere, a species that supposedly became extinct fifty million years ago. The stycosaur, during the Cretaceous period, was a twin brother of the rhinoceros, which also resembles the arsinothere, though less closely. The semiaquatic moerithere was as closely related to the hippopotamus as the fossil primate aegyptopithecus was to man, and it would be easy to confuse them in a stone carving thousands of years old.

These apparent absurdities are one of the main reasons given by conventional prehistorians for denying the great antiquity of the Ica stones.

John Rowe, an American professor, saw a stone from Dr. Cabrera's collection in Lima in about 1968. He turned it over in his hand several times, then firmly pronounced it a forgery. As was to be expected, other pundits followed his lead and decided that the Primohistoric Library of Ica did not deserve their attention.

"Conventional prehistorians," said Dr. Cabrera, "are victims of their prejudices, their blinders and their own decrees.

"People have been finding these engraved stones in the region of Ica for years, and thousands more are still undiscovered. I don't claim I can explain everything, but one thing is sure: the stones exist, and there are so many of them—perhaps a hundred thousand—that fraud can be ruled out. The fact that some of them show a man attacking a dinosaur may mean that here in Peru the ecological conditions that allowed dinosaurs to live continued until much more recent times than in the rest of the world. The fish known as the coelacanth was thought to have been extinct for hundreds of millions of years, until a living specimen of it was caught off the coast of Africa in our time."

This is an argument that cannot be dismissed lightly. Unquestionably, there are gaps in the "knowledge" of conventional prehistorians.

The geologist Neil Opdyke has noted that the disappearance of certain species of small marine organisms, radiolarians, corresponded to a period when the earth's magnetic poles shifted. The phenomenon resulted in a fifteen percent increase in radioactivity on the earth's surface, enough to disturb the dinosaurs, which had already become highly vulnerable because of their great size.

But it is known that changes in the earth's magnetic polarity affect certain areas but not others. If these changes caused dinosaurs to vanish from most of the earth, and deserts to become fertile regions and vice versa, it is logical to assume that the effects were not of the same intensity everywhere and that some dinosaurs may have been able to survive in certain areas long after the others had disappeared.

TELESCOPES AND MAGNIFYING GLASSES IN PRIMOHISTORIC* TIMES

The Primohistoric Museum of Ica contains many other fascinating wonders capable of dismaying even the most intransigent members of the Conspiracy. (*See Figures 2–5.*)

There are engravings, drawn with great precision, that show men examining objects through magnifying glasses. On other stones astronomers are observing the sky with what can only be called telescopes. Some of them are looking at a star, others at a comet with a long, radiant tail and a head represented by a ball. The star is depicted by the five-pointed figure familiar to us today, which might suggest that the drawings date from a relatively recent time. But have not stars always been seen in the shape of a pentacle?

We may speculate that the comet of Ica set off an "end of the world," either at the time of the great worldwide Deluge twelve thousand years ago, or when the "comet" Venus appeared, about five thousand years ago.

One curious observation seems to support this hypothesis. In the sky above the astronomers shown on one of the stones, there are several comets. Some are

---

* The word "prehistory" has become outmoded, since it evokes cavemen, the Iron and Bronze ages and other errors of conventional pundits. In 1962 I coined the word "primohistory"; it has the same literal meaning but evokes a new vision of ancient times that rejects the idea that man's ancestors were apes and accepts the reality of Superior Ancestors and highly advanced, vanished civilizations.

enclosed in a circle containing stars and figures resembling islands, which might be called "singular universes." One of them is heading in the direction of the earth. Between two astronomers, a drawing suggests a winged arrow with a feathered tail and a star-shaped point aimed upward. Arrow, rocket and space observatory? The interpretation may be unwarranted, but the drawing does give the impression of three simultaneous actions: the passing of a comet, astronomical observation and the upward departure of a flying object.

The top of the stone represents the sky. The comets are exceptional elements in it. The stars are of different sizes. The "singular universes," or "island universes," are open to different interpretations. They may be either clouds or islands of a submerged Earth. Their shape is in conformity with that given to dry land in other engravings.

WHAT THE ASTRONOMERS' STONE SAYS

Studied in detail, the drawings on the Astronomers' Stone (*see Figure 6*) show the following:

—Two men studying an important celestial phenomenon with the aid of a telescope.

—A flying object leaving upward.

—At least three comets drifting in a disrupted sky.

—Stars shining with unusual brightness. Some are enormous and radiant; others, probably much farther away, seem not to be involved in the cosmic disturbance.

—A vast cloud, with horizontal streaks symbolizing rain, follows the tail of an immense comet. Diluvial rains are probably falling on the earth.

—The continents, recognizable by their curves and crosshatching, are half submerged by this deluge. They look like islands.

—A star has fallen on a continent or very large island and is no longer radiating.

—In what is no doubt a major event, a boat is moving across the celestial or terrestrial ocean, carrying what appears to be three people, who may have escaped from the cataclysm.

This last interpretation may seem arbitrary but it is irresistibly suggested by the boat, the ocean, the stars, the islands and the comets.

If, in the light of traditions and mythologies, we try to put some order and logic into this puzzle* of words and images, we reach a fascinating conclusion that should be clear enough to convince many people: *the scene evokes or depicts the Deluge.* The combination of all the traditional elements supports this idea.

NO NOAH'S ARK ON MOUNT ARARAT

Such is my interpretation of the Ica stone showing astronomers with telescopes.

The flood represented may be either the worldwide Deluge or the partial flood of five thousand years ago (the flood of Ogyges and Deucalion).

Which of the two is it?

At first sight, the worldwide Deluge described by the Bible fits more naturally into the theme suggested by the engravings. It was a deluge of water, but it was set off by extraordinary atmospheric disturbances, which

---

* The puzzle is all the more perplexing because, for the ancient peoples of South America, only one mode of time existed: the present. Example: The Mayas represented the child as being born, living his adult life and dying, *simultaneously.*

The Popul Vuh, the sacred book of the ancient Mexicans, is unintelligible to us if we approach it with our usual Western thought processes, because the periods overlap, sometimes with returns or resurrections of characters who have died. The Mayas' mental structures were different from ours. The same was probably true of the Incas of San Agustin and Tiahuanaco, and the people of ancient Ica.

implies the action of comets, meteorites, storms, etc., none of which is mentioned in the Bible. And then there is that boat, that Ark, which recalls those of Noah, Xisuthros, Manu, Bochica, Coxcox, etc.

It would thus seem that the flood depicted is the worldwide Deluge that submerged the continents and destroyed Atlantis twelve thousand years ago. If so, Noah's Ark, with its cargo of *all* animal species—ants, birds, sheep, cattle, horses, lizards, dinosaurs—obviously could not have landed on the arid slopes of Mount Ararat. It had to land somewhere near grassy plains, marshes and forests, because the herbivorous dinosaurs needed enormous quantities of plant life and the carnivores needed living flesh.

We become lost in conjecture if we give credence to mythological accounts of the place where antediluvian animal life would have had a chance of survival.

THE MYSTERIOUS COMET

This hypothetical explanation of the Ica stones is attractive and offers the advantage of dating, approximately at least, one of the scenes depicted, but surprises are in store for us when we consider the partial flood of five thousand years ago.

At that time, according to tradition, there were great events in the sky. Battles between long serpents of fire were seen. Another "serpent of fire," the "bright-maned" Venus, with a horned head like that of a bull, appeared in the sky and terrified the earth's peoples.

This comet, or "fireball," which the Phoenicians called Astart, the Babylonians Ishtar and the Greeks Astarte, caused great forest fires by its intense heat. Houses and crops were also burned.

Then came the flood that brought the destruction to its climax. The scorched land was invaded by the water of overflowing rivers and tumultuous seas.

These accounts are common to nearly all the earth's peoples, as reported by Immanuel Velikovsky and Louis-Claude Vincent:

—Vala prophecy: The north pole is in the west; the sun is covered by shadows; the land sinks into the sea; the stars disappear from the sky.

—Egyptian priests: There was a great sinking of whole continents.

—Codex Chimalpopoca: Everything that existed was burned, and a rain of sandstone fell; terrifying things happened in the sky.

—Mexican traditions: Six stars fell from the sky at the time of the flood.

THE STAR THAT FELL ON THE EARTH

In the drawings on the Ica stone, particularly the star that has fallen on the continent shown at the left side of the photograph, we find a connection with an account that Paul Schliemann, grandson of the famous German archaeologist Heinrich Schliemann, related to Mu in his new mythology:

When the star Bal fell on the place where is now only sea and sky the Seven Cities with their Golden Gates and Transparent Temples quivered and shook like the leaves of a tree in a storm. And behold a flood of fire and smoke arose from the palaces. Agony and cries of the multitude filled the air. They sought refuge in their temples and citadels. And the wise Mu, the Hieratic of Ra-Mu, arose and said to them: "Did I not predict all this?" And the women and the men in their precious stones and shining garments lamented: "Mu, save us." And Mu replied: "You shall die together with your slaves and your riches and from your ashes shall rise new nations. If they forget they are

superior, not because of what they put on, but of
what they put out, the same lot will befall them!"
Flame and smoke choked the words of Mu. The
land and its inhabitants were torn to pieces and
swallowed by the depths in a few months.*

Unfortunately this text, like Churchward's Naacal tablets, has never been seen by anyone but the man who
reported it.

I do not mean to insinuate that Churchward and
Schliemann were charlatans, because the mythologies
they report are plausible; they tally with traditions and,
more startlingly, with the most recent archaeological
discoveries, such as those of Dr. Cabrera. Yet I must
emphasize that Dr. Cabrera's "tablets," which exist and
can be seen and touched, are incomparably more convincing than Churchward's.

Furthermore, the introduction of the Land of Mu
into this account, inspired by the hazardous translation
of the Troano Manuscript by Brasseur de Bourbourg,
is not accepted by all traditionalistic historians.

The Star of Bal or Baal reminds us that the Baal of
the Phoenicians (the Bel of the Assyrians, the Belin
or Belisama of the Celts) was the god and representa-
tive on Earth of the planet Venus. The star in question,

---

* Compare with the Book of Revelation in the New Testament,
where, in Chapter 8, when the seventh seal was broken, "there came
hail and fire mingled with blood, and this was hurled upon the earth.
A third of the earth was burnt, a third of the trees were burnt, all the
green grass was burnt.

"The second angel blew his trumpet; and what looked like a great
blazing mountain was hurled into the sea. A third of the sea was
turned to blood, a third of the living creatures in it died, and a third
of the ships on it foundered.

"The third angel blew his trumpet; and a great star shot from the
sky, flaming like a torch; and it fell on a third of the rivers and
springs. The name of the star was Wormwood...."

This green star—green like wormwood—does not belong to future
times, but to the past time when the green Star of Baal, or Venus,
engendered terrifying cataclysms. The prophet's vision is related not
to the future, but to the past.

which can also be related to that of the Hebrews, more logically suggests the cataclysm that destroyed Atlantis.

To sum up, we can see the Astronomers' Stone as depicting either the great mythological Deluge or the fall of the star reported by the manuscript seen or invented by Paul Schliemann. I am more inclined toward the worldwide Deluge, because of the boat or Ark transporting escapees. This would give an age of twelve thousand years to the Primohistoric Library of Ica.

But it is probable that "destructions of the world" obey cyclical laws. If so, the events associated with Noah's Ark and the Star of Baal are repeated at fixed intervals (the figure of twenty-one thousand years has been put forward) in about the same way, and give rise to the same traditions. The Astronomers' Stone may thus have an age of twenty-one thousand multiplied by x years.

ATLANTIS HUNDREDS OF MILLIONS OF YEARS AGO

Two rounded black andesite stones, weighing about two hundred pounds, bear a certain relation to the Astronomers' Stone. They seem to depict an immense ocean ringed by high mountains or a river that takes up half the drawing. Four continents are drifting on the oceans. They bear representations of people, animals, houses and mountains, which should help to identify them. (*See Figures 7 and 8.*)

Here again, imagination calls on mythology in an effort to find a solution to the enigma, and we think of the earth as it was hundreds of millions of years ago, when, according to Wegner's theory, the continents were adrift on the magma surrounding the globe.

On Continent C, identified as South America by Dr. Cabrera, we see a face of the same type as those on the Ica stones, but it seems to me that Continent E, with its high mountains (the Andes?) and its llama, is equally well suited to represent South America. Note the depiction of a house with a roof, a door and a window exactly like houses in our own time. The lakes, circles, crosses and stars scattered over the continents have a precise meaning that escapes us.

To me, Atlantis—and this is only a timid hypothesis—is at G, where we clearly see two high mountain peaks, a kind of sea creature with a tail, carrying a fish, and an unusual house. Is this the fabulous continent that was submerged in the Atlantic, according to Plato? Or is it at C, or elsewhere?

Figures E and F are so enigmatic that we can only make precarious conjectures about them.

FIGHTS BETWEEN MEN AND DINOSAURS

Extinct monsters are engraved on many of the Ica stones. The photograph (see Figure 9) shows an image of what may be a brachiosaur, the largest of the dinosaurs. It was eighty feet long, weighed up to fifty tons and lived a hundred and forty million years ago, at the most. However, the triangular bony plates along its back suggest that it may be a sauropelta (length eighteen feet, weight three tons), or perhaps a spinosaur, two to three times longer and twice as heavy.

Two men wearing loincloths have attacked the monster by climbing on its back. One of them is striking its head with an axe, the other is stabbing it in the back. A kind of humanoid, with a tail, seems to have fallen off after an unsuccessful attack. This species of primate is totally unknown to anthropologists and zoologists. Perhaps it belonged to a vanished link, or a nonviable type in evolution.* It should be noted that the Ances-

* My friend and correspondent Yves Morel, who lives in Tahiti, says that in the high mountains of South Vietnam there is a population of hairy people with very large heads, hands and legs. They are

tors of that time knew how to smelt metals, because the axe and the knife obviously have metal blades.

On the left-hand stone is an animal that may be an amphibian, the dendrerpeton (ten inches long). On the right-hand stone is one of the earliest known birds, the archaeopteryx. It was the size of a crow and lived a hundred and eighty million years ago.

PRIMATE SERVANTS OF MAN

The humanoid shown falling off the monster poses a problem capable of disrupting our view of human genesis: the contemporaneity of *Homo sapiens* and links that seem to relate him either to a hominid or to a kind of fish-man represented in mythology by Oannes, the god and civilizer of the peoples of Babylonia. He was the Janus of the Romans and the Prometheus of the Greeks. He was shown as being half-man and half-fish (he was also said to be half-frog), with a tail. He came out of the sea each morning to impart knowledge to human beings. (Etymology: Oannes, Oan, Ogen, Okean, Okeanos, Oceanos.)

It is disturbing to note the resemblance between ancient depictions of the Chaldean initiator and the primates on the Ica stones—and the resemblance of both to a fetus in its mother's womb.

The humanoid falling from the dinosaur has three important features: his tail, his elongated face and his four-fingered hands. Not enough attention has been paid to the mystery of four-fingered hands, which is almost never encountered outside the lands of the Incas. Orejona, the mother goddess who landed at Lake Titicaca, had four fingers on each hand and four toes

---

cannibals, and greatly feared by the Mois. They all have small tails, one to two inches long.

A Vietnamese friend of Morel's, now living in Papeete, saw several of those people: they worked on her mother's plantation, after being captured by Mois.

on each foot. The central god and the other personages on the Gate of the Sun at Tiahuanaco also have four-fingered hands. This suggests a human race alien to Earth, or not yet completely detached from its original type.

(A computer study has concluded that in two hundred and fifty years man will be about five inches taller, on the average, will no longer have wisdom teeth, will be nearly twice as intelligent, and will have only four toes on each foot, the little toe having completely atrophied.)

In the photograph (*see Figure 10*), the primates have five-fingered hands, which may be webbed, and no thumbs. Their tails are like those of dinosaurs. Their heads suggest a mammal (left) and a shark (right). I regret not finding any resemblance between them and the enigmatic dolphin.

Were these primates amphibians? There is reason to think so. Many of the Ica stones show them as attentive helpers of human beings. They may have been man's ancestors in an evolutionary system where links developed at uneven rates.

These nonhuman helpers make us think of monkeys, which have been regressing for the past four thousand years, but fulfilled the functions of sailors and servants among the ancient Egyptians. Baboons and long-tailed monkeys are said to have worked in the rigging of Queen Hatshepsut's ships when she left the land of Punt. It is thought that monkeys also watched over children and climbed trees to pick fruit beyond the reach of gardeners.

The *Dictionnaire de la Civilisation Egyptienne* tells us that in the time of the Theban Second Empire the monkey "learned to understand what was said to him as soon as he was brought from Ethiopia, and pedants claimed that he was more malleable than an Egyptian schoolboy."

In ancient times a kind of monkey called the *cebus* was known. Pliny the naturalist writes about it as follows: "An Ethiopian animal named the *cebus* was also seen at the games of the great Pompey. Its hind legs looked like the feet and legs of a man, and its front feet resembled hands. Since that time, those animals have not been seen again in Rome."

Pythagoras mentions a superior monkey known as the *kepos,* which lived on the shore of the Red Sea.

AMEGHINO'S *HOMUNCULUS PATAGONICUS*

In the nineteenth century an Argentinian paleontologist named Florentino Ameghino maintained that South America was the birthplace of the human race. At that time, prehistorians placed mankind's origin in Asia; they now place it in Africa. Still, the people and hominids of ancient Ica seem to lend strong support to Ameghino's view that man originated in South America in the middle of the Tertiary.

According to him, our ancestor, whom he named *Homunculus patagonicus,* was smaller than we are and had the form of an animal. Between *Homunculus patagonicus* and modern man was a series of links: the *prothomos* (premen).

Ameghino based his theory on several bones, including a femur and a cervical vertebra found at Monte Hermoso in the province of Buenos Aires. He explained the peopling of the globe by stating that South American man had gone north after the formation of the Isthmus of Panama, and into Asia by way of the Bering Strait. Europe was populated by means of the land bridge between Canada and Europe at the beginning of the Pleistocene.

A CESAREAN WITH ANESTHESIA

As a surgeon, Dr. Cabrera takes particular pride in some of his stones that prove the biological knowledge of our Superior Ancestors. These are the most amazing and valuable stones in his collection, for while the others present images of the past, these reveal secrets of the surgery of tomorrow.

During the late afternoon I spent in Dr. Cabrera's fantastic museum, I obviously did not have time to examine all of the eleven thousand engraved stones that it contains. I could only look them over, without noting more than a few of their details.

When I took a picture of Dr. Cabrera beside a portrait of his ancestor Jeronimo Luis (*see Figure 11*), my camera, unknown to me, recorded an image that I did not discover until later. And what an image! It shows a cesarean operation that, says Dr. Cabrera, was depicted on stone sixty million years ago.

There are dozens of stones in the photograph, on shelves and on the floor. The largest of them, in the lower left-hand corner, gives the details of the operation. (*See Figures 12, 13 and 14.*)

ORGAN TRANSPLANTS
IN PRIMOHISTORIC TIMES

It seems that prehistoric surgeons achieved positive results in cases where our best modern specialists encounter hazards and depressing uncertainties. Precise engravings forcefully assure us that heart, kidney and even brain transplants were successfully performed thousands or perhaps millions of years ago.

I am not qualified to give a scientific opinion on this subject, so I will limit myself to describing and interpreting, to the best of my ability, the images I brought back from Ica. Dr. Cabrera, an eminent surgeon and an erudite prehistorian, will evaluate them in the book he is now writing, a book that will probably be a milestone in the history of mankind.

In fourteen astonishing images we will see the prehistoric technique by which a heart was completely replaced, including its arteriovenous vessels.

CHAPTER 2

∞∞

A Heart Transplant
in Fourteen Images

IN THE FOURTH CHAPTER of my book *Forgotten Worlds*
I described the discovery, according to the report of the
Marmajaijan expedition into central Asia, of eight
skeletons showing traces of surgical operations in the
chest cavity. The operations were performed a hundred
thousand years ago and were successful, judging from
the thickness of the periosteum. Professor Leonidov
Marmajaijan's conclusions made it possible to establish
that, after resection of the ribs, a heart must have been
transplanted.

In the Ica collection the procedure of such an operation is engraved on about twenty stones. (*See Figures
15 through 28.*) These engravings are eloquent enough
to convince us that the Superior Ancestors of Ica had
extensive biological knowledge and were really capable
of performing heart transplants.

The preoperative phases and certain features of the

operation itself made Dr. Cabrera realize that the phenomenon of rejection was probably prevented by means of the special properties possessed by the blood of a pregnant woman. This blood undoubtedly contains an active ingredient or an antirejection hormone whose absence is the cause of genetic incompatibility (spontaneous abortion). Its abrupt diminution at the end of pregnancy may trigger the process of childbirth.

The antirejection hormone, says Dr. Cabrera, must be sought in the blood of pregnant women between the third and fifth months, which is the best period of activity.

The fact that blood from a pregnant woman was used in transplant operations leads us to assume that the Superior Ancestors had knowledge enabling them to overcome the phenomenon of rejection.

AND EVEN A BRAIN TRANSPLANT?

My first visit to the Primohistoric Museum of Ica was short, because I was not expecting such an important discovery, and also because we had to go on to Paracas and then to Lima, where we had reservations for a flight to Colombia, our final destination being the prestigious archaeological site of San Agustin. It would have taken several days to make a comprehensive examination of Dr. Cabrera's prodigious collection. I had to wait till my longer visit in March of the following year.

Another stroke of bad luck was that I had only one flash lamp and it stopped working when I had taken nineteen pictures. But among them I was surprised to find two that showed a brain transplant, according to what I was told by Dr. Cabrera. He later sent me some of his own photographs, and I took more during my next visit to Ica.

The brain transplant is illustrated on several stones. My photographs (see Figures 29, 30 and 31) did not turn out very well, but Dr. Cabrera's book will describe the operation in detail. The most optimistic of our modern surgeons believe that it will eventually be possible to replace all the organs of the human body, except the brain.

INSCRIPTION FOR A GREAT INITIATE

Thousands and thousands of engravings still beckoned to our curiosity, but for the moment we had absorbed our fill of wonders on that memorable day. It was time to go on to our Colombian adventures. We were not going to leave the Andes but we had to tear ourselves away from the magic of our host. He insisted that we write in his visitors' book. I will here reproduce what I wrote, because it shows the depth of my amazement.

Today, April 29, 1973, Dr. Cabrera Darquea opened for me the book of mankind's fantastic past. It is a discovery and a revelation that will influence my thinking from now on, and probably that of my readers also.

Dr. Cabrera Darquea is the greatest discoverer not only of our century, but of all time. In a few years, his ideas and his museum of stones will open the era of the real knowledge that has so far been hidden from us by conspiracies of falsehood. I will be proud to be his disciple, if he is willing, and I here express all my admiration and affection for him.

R. CHARROUX

WITNESSES TO THE INCREDIBLE

The discovery of Dr. Cabrera's secret museum, and especially the fantastic history of the world suggested by the stones, seemed so astounding that I realized how difficult it would be to make prehistorians and the general public accept them. Even with the support of photographs it was a strange adventure that might give rise to doubt, if not incredulity.

That was why in March 1974, when I left on a trip that would eventually take me to Mexico, I insisted that Robert Laffont, my publisher, and Francis Mazière, the editor in charge of the series in which my books appear, come to Peru with me. On March 12 and 13 they were in Dr. Cabrera's museum and examined the stones at leisure. (*See Figure 32.*) On the fourteenth they walked on the *pistas* of the Nascan Desert. On the fifteenth they saw the Candlestick of the Andes.

In Ica inspection of the stones took place in the presence of several witnesses, including Colonel Omar Chioino Carranza, director of the Peruvian Aeronautical Museum, and Edmond Borit of Ica, both of whom accompanied us to all the sites. Besides those witnesses, I can also mention the names of Professor Alejandro Pezzia, curator of the Ica Museum, which has about fifty stones, the agricultural engineer Alain Elias and J. J. P. Van Hemelrijck, manager of the Hotel Turista.

I think Colonel Omar Chioino Carranza summed up the opinion of these witnesses when he stated, "There are at least twenty thousand of those engraved stones, and probably many more. They are very old and it is impossible for us to doubt that they are perfectly genuine."

CHAPTER 3

☙☙

The Conspiracy
of Conventional Minds

EIGHT YEARS OF STUDY and reflection have enabled Dr.
Cabrera to elaborate views that differ from those of
prehistorians but will sooner or later be substituted for
them in official teachings, because truth must someday
rise to the surface as oil rises in water.

According to Dr. Cabrera, the first human being
came from a selective mutation in the primate stock
that originated the biological group of the most intelligent animals. Man does not, then, descend from the
monkey, and his appearance was a unique event in
earthly evolution.

LONG-TAILED HUMAN BEINGS

The first human beings had elongated faces, tails
that hung down to the ground and hands with long,
slender thumbs. That is what the Ica stones teach us.

"I reject the very vague possibility that those primitive people may have been taught by initiates or intel-

ligent, superior beings from other planets," says Dr. Cabrera. I cannot follow my friend and teacher in that assertion, because it would mean rejecting the basis of mythology and the probability calculations of the most highly advanced astronomers of our time.

According to Professor Pierre Guérin, we may assume that there are half a million intelligent societies in our galaxy, most of which are millions or billions of years ahead of us in science and technology. As for the mysterious flying objects that have been seen in the sky by tens of thousands of people, the climate of opinion is becoming more favorable to accepting the idea of messages from extraterrestrial beings, and even contacts with them. Dr. Emerson Schildeler has stated that he does not believe all UFOs (Unidentified Flying Objects) come from our planet.

The Belgian magazine *Bufoi* gives the following list of scientists who attended a conference at the University of Arizona in 1971, and who accept the existence of UFOs: Dr. Allen Hynek, Dr. Robert Creegan, Dr. Leo Sprinkel, Dr. Emerson Schildeler, Dr. John Munday, Dr. Frank Salisbury, all professors at American universities. They believe that some UFOs are controlled by beings from space.

Like Dr. Cabrera, I believe that *primitive* man was essentially similar to native earthly man, but I do not rule out the possibility of intervention by Instructors from another planet.

Actually, this problem is not basically that of Superior Ancestors; it lies, rather, in the age that should be assigned to the first intellectually advanced human beings on our planet.

MAN WAS BORN
THIRTY MILLION YEARS AGO

Man was not born a million years ago, as was thought until recently: he existed 2.8 million years ago in Kenya, east of Lake Rudolf, and it is certain that much older remains of *Homo habilis* or *Homo sapiens* will be found in some other part of the world.

Conventional prehistorians present these stages in man's development:

Ramapithecus: a primate on the way to humanization; fourteen million years ago.

Australopithecus: already human; crude tools; five million years ago.

Kenya Man: well-made tools; two million years ago.

Homo erectus: physically similar to us; one million years ago.

Homo sapiens: eighty to a hundred thousand years ago, though some writers say two hundred thousand.

Other, more realistic prehistorians and anthropologists, go much further in their assertions. Professor A. Delmas of the Paris Academy of Medicine, for example, states that the first human beings appeared at least thirty million years ago. Why? Because our upright posture could have become natural only after tens of millions of years; because we have longer legs and shorter arms than apes; because the shape, orientation and capacity of our skulls are fundamentally different from those of apes.

And Professor Delmas concludes: "Four-footed walking, brachiation (swinging from branch to branch) and two-footed walking apparently should not be viewed as successive stages in evolution, but as very old and rather exclusive specializations."*

COLONIZING EXTRATERRESTRIALS

Professor Delmas' views imply a human adventure not of the kind that has been rashly decreed by pre-

---

* Near the Ethiopian village of Dessye, about two hundred miles northeast of Addis Ababa, the American paleontologist Dr. Carl Johanson discovered fossilized bones of a man who walked upright more than three million years ago.

historians, but one in conformity with the ideas I have always advocated:

—If human beings have been on our planet for thirty million years, they must have developed advanced civilizations that have unfortunately been lost or veiled by time and geological cataclysms.

—We had Superior Ancestors. This is the most probable hypothesis. Nevertheless, even though I do not believe it, I cannot rule out the hypothesis of an antediluvian earth from which intelligent native man was absent. To explain the development of civilization, we must then envision a colonization by people from another planet. In that case, the first human beings came here millions of years ago from a remote planet that may even have been outside our known universe.

Once we manage to see beyond the outdated theories of conventional prehistorians, we obtain a new view of the past, one that takes full account of man's obvious superiority over other animals. The basic difference between man and other animals seems to lie in the phenomenon of projection—the ability to imagine and foresee—which is much more clearly perceptible in man. Man is better able than animals to integrate his mind into the space-time continuum.

The fantastic primohistory that I want to substitute for fossil prehistory is more probable and authentic.

DOCUMENTS AND VESTIGES THAT WANT TO SPEAK

For more than three thousand years the sacred books of India, the Nordic countries and the Celtic West, supported by traditions and writings from Plato to Eugène Beauvois, have been saying that some of our ancestors were cultivated people who developed civilizations equal or superior to ours in certain respects. Unfortunately the traces left by those people of ancient times are rare, ambiguous and fragile, and conventional prehistorians have never deigned to give them their learned attention.

It was known, through traditions and graphic representations, that gods who came from the planet Venus had reigned in Mexico, Phoenicia and Babylonia. Very old Indian writings (Mahavira, Drona Parva) stated that the gods fought an atomic war against each other, that they had flying machines that carried them through the air and even to the stars, that they had astronomical observatories and performed the most delicate surgical operations. All this was nothing but imagination, said the guardians of "true" science.

Other discoveries: a depiction of a space rocket piloted by an astronaut on the Palenque slab in Mexico; codices describing jet aircraft; the engraved disks in the caves of Baian-Kara-Ula in Tibet, which were left there by ancient astronauts, according to the translations of Professor Tsum-Um-Nui of the Peking Academy. Imagination, said the official pundits.

And with the same virtuous indignation they rejected Tiahuanaco, Moses' Ark-condenser and the electric light used by Rabbi Jechiele in the time of Saint Louis.*

"All that is nothing but wild speculation," they objected. "A civilization can't be recognized and accepted unless we find documents, structures, carved stones—in short, something substantial that can be scientifically evaluated."

"What about Atlantis?"

"Another daydream! It comes from people's need to invent Superior Ancestors for themselves. We have no reason to believe that the Atlanteans, if they ever existed, developed a science on the same level as ours."

Those stern rationalists were not wrong on every point. It must be acknowledged, even with what we have

---

* I have described all these things in my books *One Hundred Thousand Years of Man's Unknown History, Legacy of the Gods* and *Masters of the World*.

learned from the Ica stones, that no ancient civilization—Egypt, the Inca Empire, Mexico, Lepenski Vir,
Medzamor—reached the stage of the airplane, the automobile, railroads, computers, etc., if we base our judgment on documents now known. Yet recent discoveries
of undersea ruins off the coast of Bimini in the Bahamas
prove that the Atlantic has swallowed up unknown
cities, and perhaps even a whole civilization.

A PAINFUL CHOICE:
A CHRISTIAN OR AN ARCHAEOLOGIST?

Archaeologists, geologists and prehistorians vehemently rejected everything that contradicted their sacrosanct assumptions. Although those of them who pro-
fessed to be Christians acknowledged the Biblical
Deluge and Jesus Christ, if they were questioned persistently, on a strictly scientific level, they denied that
those legends should be taken seriously.* But they refused to let themselves be quoted because they did not
want such heretical words to reach the ears of the
religious leaders and wealthy people on whom their
advancement depended.

It is not easy for a conventional prehistorian to believe that man was created by Jehovah and that he
descends from an anthropoid; that the stars were placed
in the sky to light our earth and that our planet is a
minute speck of dust in the cosmos; that the universe
was created by God a few thousand years ago and by a
"big bang" billions of years ago; that our first ancestors,
Adam and Eve, lived in an earthly paradise and that

---

* A distinction must be made here. All ancient peoples, and tradi-
tions all over the world, attest to the reality of the Deluge. (See
Worlds in Collision, by Immanuel Velikovsky.) The nonexistence of
Jesus Christ, however, is proved by Egyptian papyruses dating from
1500 B.C. that relate the same things as the Gospels. (See my book
The Mysterious Past.)

their lives were poor and precarious, exposed to all the dangers of a hostile environment.

Even so, respectable scholars have stated categorically that prehistoric people lived in caves, wore animal skins and invented bronze thirty-five hundred years ago. Then, without retracting a thing, they blithely went off to discover, at Lepenski Vir, Yugoslavia, villages skillfully built ten thousand years ago, and at Medzamor, Soviet Armenia, factories dating from a time when prehistoric people, supposedly armed with clubs and stone axes, made eighteen varieties of bronze sixty-five hundred years before they were said to have invented it.

THEY ACTUALLY KNOW VERY LITTLE

A coelacanth was caught off the coast of Africa.

"Impossible!" decreed the Conspiracy. "That species became extinct two hundred million years ago."

"And dinosaurs?"

"They disappeared sixty million years ago."

"But what about the discovery of. . . ."

"You're only trying to make a name for yourself as a nonconformist!"

"Glozel—there's one thing you can't deny."

"Glozel? Never heard of it."

"What do you think of the Candlestick of the Andes and the lines in the Nascan Desert?"

At this point the learned gentlemen sensed a trap and cautiously backed off, for the Candlestick of the Andes and the Nascan Desert markings are absolutely unknown in prehistory and archaeology.

Think of it: those drawings spread over hundreds of miles remain unnoticed by people with huge sums of money at their disposal for research!

But the members of the Conspiracy really see red when someone without the proper academic credentials has the audacity to discover an archaeological site, an unknown city, a submerged temple or tablets and pottery from an unknown civilization. The call to battle goes up in dusty museums and the conference rooms of archaeological societies.

"It's a fraud!" cry the outraged defenders of orthodoxy.

And they prepare to loose their thunderbolts at the insolent outsider who has dared to climb the Andes or dive into the Atlantic to find an archaeological site *which they alone are entitled to discover.*

Poor Boucher de Perthes, Champollion, Schliemann, Marcelino de Sautuola, Emile Fradin and Dr. Morlet— what affronts and humiliations you had to endure before the Conspiracy surrendered!

THE CONSPIRACY AGAINST GLOZEL

Fortunately prehistorians of the new generation have broken with the ways of their predecessors. They know that caves were only occasional dwellings, that clothes —hats, jackets, trousers, shoes—existed twenty thousand years ago, that people of the Magdalenian (fifteen to thirty thousand years ago) had mental structures like ours, that they were capable of reflecting, devising plans, writing and calculating, that they knew how to sculpt, draw, paint, study the sky, smelt metals, make boats and perform surgical operations.

Other prehistorians go even further and regard the people of ancient times, even as long as thirty thousand years ago, as advanced ancestors who built cities and traveled from continent to continent, with brains more highly developed than ours, better able to grasp the mysteries of the unknown and the intricacies of mathematics and philosophy.

The gap between the two schools of thought is so great that as early as 1930, with regard to the Glozel Museum, A. Bjorn, curator of the Museum of Oslo, said indignantly, "One must be blind and dishonest to deny the authenticity of Glozel." A. Mendes-Correa, professor of anthropology and dean of the faculty of science at the University of Oporto, wrote in reference to the French Conspiracy, "In the future, people will be amazed at the incredible glibness with which arrogance and hatred of change invented arguments against the obvious facts."

And an honest man, A. Desforges, a charter member of the French Prehistorical Society, summed up the opinion of genuine prehistorians in these terms: "Scientists are divided into two categories: those who work and those who live from the work of others."

Archaeologists in the first group, those who are accustomed to making excavations, have always upheld the authenticity of Glozel. The others have tried to discredit a discovery *that they were not allowed to exploit.*

VILIFIED ARCHAEOLOGISTS

Here are some of the heroes who have devoted their genius and strength to the cause of archaeology, and who have been called counterfeiters, swindlers and charlatans:

Plato, the first to reveal the existence of Atlantis.

Heinrich Schliemann, discoverer of Troy. Official prehistorians called him a dilettante and a hoaxer, and wrote ninety defamatory booklets against him in the space of a few years.

Jean-François Champollion, who was desperately poor and nearly died of cold and hunger in his attic room. After enduring countless humiliations, losing his job as a teacher and being exiled for "high treason," he deciphered the Rosetta Stone and translated the Egyptian hieroglyphics. He died in obscurity and justice was not done to him till sixty-four years after his death.

Emile Beauvois, a scholar in the early part of this

century, one of the greatest figures of protohistory. He wrote on Thule, pre-Columbian America, the Celts, the Atlantic islands, etc. His works, along with those of Herodotus and Velikovsky, form the most valuable exposition of ancient civilizations. They were vehemently contested and are still relatively unknown.

Marcelino de Sautuola, who discovered the admirable cave paintings of Altamira, in Spain. He had to struggle against the Conspiracy all his life to have them recognized as genuine.

Immanuel Velikovsky, the originator of avant-garde prehistory, disrupted the absurd theories of his contemporaries and restored logical order to the great cosmic events that cast light on ancient civilizations and mankind's past. He was violently opposed by official scientists. His major book, *Worlds in Collision,* is a veritable bible for researchers.

Emile Fradin and *Dr. Antonin Morlet* of Vichy, France, discoverers of the Glozel civilization, which is now accepted all over the world, had to struggle for fifty years against conspiracies of hatred and slander that wanted either to steal their discovery or discredit it.

And today abuse is heaped on *Louis-Claude Vincent,* a professor at the Paris School of Anthropology who believes in the antediluvian continent of Mu and supports my views and discoveries. (Some of my readers may know that I have the honor of being unofficially banned from French television and radio. I am periodically insulted and slandered on certain programs, without being given a chance to answer.)

AN EXPLODED PLANET

The doctrines of prehistorians are nearly always wrong, and their books are as outdated as medieval coats of mail. In our time, it should be recognized that the ancient civilizations of Mu and Atlantis disappeared in an immense cataclysm, probably caused by a noxious science brought to them "from the sky" by Instructors now called angels or gods.

Had they asked for help from those "angels," or were they their victims? The people of the twentieth century, who have learned more in the last fifty years than was learned during the previous three thousand, would like to know the answer to that question.

The geometric progression of our knowledge implies that in a hundred years its present level will be surpassed to such an extent that we cannot yet imagine it. There is no reason not to believe that we will be given the benefit of the supposedly fantastic science of the "space people," or that we will become the interplanetary Instructors of a people less advanced than we are. This latter possibility is seldom emphasized by Ufologists, yet our whole space industry has the goal of reaching other planets and perhaps contacting other intelligent beings in our galaxy. And while there is no conclusive evidence that flying saucers have landed on Earth, it is certain that well-identified flying objects have left Earth and passed near other heavenly bodies or landed on them.

It is perhaps symptomatic of the approach of apocalyptic times that we are more interested in possible past events than in the frightening future events that lie in store for us. Or that, in an effort to convince ourselves that salvation will come from space visitors, we do our best to believe that the same thing happened to our remote ancestors.

But what will probably be possible in the twenty-first century must have presented enormous difficulties to the beings who, I believe, came to our planet from an alien civilization twelve thousand and five thousand years ago. (I have presented this view in several of my books, notably *Legacy of the Gods*.) Those extraterrestrials, confronted with societies at a low stage of development, were scarcely tempted to prolong their stay on our planet. Nevertheless, everything indicates that they came here, taught our ancestors enough to enable them to create the first civilizations, and then either returned to their own planet or merged into the Earth's population.

They may have come from a distant solar system or, more likely, from the planet that once occupied the orbit of the asteroids, about a hundred and twenty million miles from Earth. When that planet exploded, one of its fragments may have been the "comet of fire," described by ancient peoples, which was captured and stabilized by our sun and became the planet Venus five thousand years ago.

TRUTH WILL OUT

Such are the elements at our disposal for imagining our unknown history. "There is nothing covered up that will not be uncovered, nothing hidden that will not be made known," says the Bible (Matthew 10:26).* Suddenly documents came out of their secret hiding places, dazzling, amazing, irrefutable.

It was an Initiate who brought the revelation of our unknown history: Dr. Javier Cabrera Darquea, of Ica, Peru, at the edge of the magic pampa where straight lines and giant drawings, visible only from the air, presented a baffling enigma to archaeologists.

We are now beginning to envisage the remote past and identify those Superior Ancestors of whom we formerly spoke only intuitively and in the uncertain light of mythology.

1. It seems that man is not descended from the ape, since he lived, if not before the anthropoids, at least

* All Biblical quotations are from *The New English Bible,* Oxford University Press, 1970. (Translator's note.)

at the same time as humanoids with tails who were closer to saurians or fish than to gibbons or orangutangs.

2. Initiators very probably came from the sky.

3. They instructed ancient peoples and made them into the Superior Ancestors—Atlanteans or Pre-Atlanteans—to whom we have been referring.

Judging from the Ica stones, the Nasca drawings and the legacies of Egypt, the Inca Empire, Mexico, Lepenski Vir, Medzamor, etc., those Great Ancestors developed advanced civilizations but never used the wheel, which was taboo, and therefore could not invent airplanes, computers, automobiles, railroads, etc. The source of that taboo remains a mystery, but it is certain that antediluvian civilizations took a path different from ours.

This summary, however conjectural, was necessary before we could approach the mysteries of the Nascan Desert and the Primohistoric Library of Ica.

CHAPTER 4

The Legacy of the Atlanteans

"WE ARE ON THE EVE of a great battle," Heinrich Schliemann is said to have remarked when he discovered Troy. It is just as likely that the "Ica affair" will stir up many controversies, overthrow many theories and scandalize prehistorians and archaeologists of the old school.

What? Civilization was not born in Sumer? Not even in India, Egypt or Phoenicia? How can the pundits of the Conspiracy pursue their placid meditations if some troublemaker throws firecrackers under their chairs?

It will be a long, long time before prehistorians go to Ica from Paris, Rome, London or New York. It took ten years for an eminent French prehistorian to go from Poitiers (by bicycle) to the marvelous field of flint tools at Le Grand Pressigny. Most French specialists have never deigned to go and see the Glozel Museum. The Nascan Desert markings? They are unknown to archaeologists, since they cannot be seen from an armchair. So a lot of water will flow under the bridge before those respectable gentlemen bestir themselves to visit Dr. Cabrera's primohistoric museum!

Ah, the power of inertia, animosity, dishonesty and ignorance!

THE HIDING PLACES
ARE NEAR OCUCAJE

Dr. Cabrera does not ask for blind, unreasoning trust. On the contrary, he demands examination of his stones by many experts, with all proper precautions and scrupulous honesty.

On the subject of where the stones were discovered, he speaks frankly:

"Experts should obviously be the first to go to the site. But I would like a delay, for the following reasons. I've gathered eleven thousand stones but there are still many more and I want to make my collection as complete as possible. If the hiding place becomes known, tourists and curious amateurs will flock to it and take away many of the stones. The unity of the collection will then be destroyed. So first there must be a committee of experts, of which I, of course, will be a member.* And the Peruvian government must preserve the site by keeping it under guard."

The fact is that the location of the site is known to within a few miles.

The engraved stones are andesite, an eruptive rock about eighty million years old. They are coated with a

---

* Dr. Cabrera is right to be mistrustful. If he reveals the location of the hiding places, unscrupulous prehistorians will take over his discovery and credit for it will go to them. Who benefited from the discovery of the Lascaux caves and the prehistoric library of Lussac-les-Châteaux? Not the discoverers!

thick layer of oxidation that covers the engravings and proves their authenticity.

It is up to Dr. Cabrera to reveal the exact location of the site, but, to give the reader an approximate idea, I will say that the stones are found about twenty miles south-southwest of Ica, near Ocucaje and the Rio Ica, in graves and sanctuary caves. This is a semidesert region, richer in stony pampas than in pastureland. Yet this is where the people of ancient times chose to establish the memory center of earthly history.

The prodigious Nascan Desert markings had been known for more than twenty years before anyone in Peru took an interest in them. Similarly, interest in the Ica stones has not been aroused all at once.

HUAQUEROS AND PILLAGERS

The first collectors were, in about 1955, the brothers Carlos and Pablo Soldi, who lived in the hacienda of Ocucaje, near the place where peasants say they first found engraved stones. Carlos died in 1967, Pablo in 1968, and the 114 stones in their possession were given to the regional museum in Ica.

At about the same time as the Soldi brothers, Commander Elias, curator of the Callao Naval Museum till 1973, bought stones from the Ocucaje peasants. He had nearly three hundred of them in his museum.

The architect Santiago Agurto Calvo, former rector of the National University of Engineering and a man with a passionate interest in archaeology, carried out excavations in conjunction with Professor Alejandro Pezzia, curator of the Ica Museum. They found three engraved stones in pre-Columbian graves not far from the Soldi brothers' hacienda. Their discovery was reported in the journal of the museum and in the magazine *Dominical* of the newspaper *El Comercio* on December 11, 1966.

These archaeologists were collectors; they did not venture very far into study of the stones but they had the great merit of working to demonstrate their authenticity, which was acknowledged by Santiago Agurto.

It is certain that since 1965 many amateurs, enlightened or otherwise, have taken advantage of the negligence of the Peruvian cultural authorities to remove hundreds of engraved stones from the country. Those stones cannot now be recovered, and their absence seriously diminishes the unity of Dr. Cabrera's collection.

His first stone, given to him by his friend Felix Lhona, was no doubt found by a peasant, a *huaquero* (seeker of ancient pottery) or a shepherd who had searched the rocky shelters in the cliff along the Rio Ica.

Where did this stone come from? Its source was not revealed, probably because the peasants or *huaqueros* who had found the site wanted to exploit it themselves by selling stones to amateur archaeologists.

The first discoverer is rumored to have been an Ocucaje gravedigger, in 1960.

A VILLAGE IN THE DESERT

On the highway from Ica to Palpa, at kilometer marker 325, a large sign announces that Ocucaje is to the right. A little road branches off from the highway and leads toward the mountains, through fields of cotton and corn. This does not last long, however: the road soon changes into a trail, then vanishes into a desert.

For a time we felt as if we were in the middle of the Sahara. Then, after going around a mountain, we saw Ocucaje, a village of about twenty little houses scattered over the bleak, treeless pampa. (*See Figure 33.*)

The arrival of our car caused a sensation. We were

quickly surrounded by a throng of children. They had realized the purpose of our visit and we were surely not the first "tourists" to come there. Little girls tugged at our sleeves, trying to pull us toward their houses, and asked if we wanted stones.

We wanted to see Ocucaje, out of curiosity, but we did not expect or want to discover the secret so closely guarded by Dr. Cabrera. I ask him to forgive us: we did not unveil Ocucaje, it unveiled itself to us.

There is no longer any need for secrecy, since Dr. Cabrera's book will soon be published, and since everyone in Ica knows where the stones come from.

"They're found in the countryside around Ocucaje," Professor Alejandro Pezzia had told us. "All the peasants have some, and they even sell them."

It was an open secret, but how could Dr. Cabrera have been told that fact without distressing him as a collector and an archaeologist? Anyone could go to Ocucaje, offer a sizable sum of money and take precious volumes away from his primohistoric library, and from Peru. We had no desire to play the part of vandals, but the fact is that as soon as we were in the middle of the village we were assailed by people who wanted to sell us stones and pottery.

ENGRAVED STONES
EVEN IN POULTRY YARDS

Every home has a large number of black andesite stones that were engraved thousands of years ago with drawings of animals and human beings. (They are actually gray or ocher, with a dark patina, but, hoping to make them more attractive, the peasants accentuate the patina with black shoe polish.) Huge engraved stones lie in the little adjoining gardens protected from the wind and sand by reed fences. Chickens perch on some of them and ducklings look for food in their uncertain shade. (*See Figure 34.*)

All the villagers obviously know where the ancient messages are buried, and most of them rely mainly on working as *huaqueros* for their livelihood.

We did not try to find out where the site is. It is undoubtedly near the village, and still mysterious, which will help to safeguard the stones for at least a little longer.

There are prodigious archaeological riches in the surrounding area, including a cemetery of painted ceramics. We were offered valuable specimens from it but we refused to buy them. That pottery is only two to three thousand years old. Does it date from the same time as the engraved stones? Is it buried in the same hiding place? It is up to Dr. Cabrera and the Peruvian authorities to investigate those questions.

Our friend Francis Mazière, who was the first to visit the *huaqueros,* in March 1974, can testify to the authenticity of the stones. The Ocucaje villagers unquestionably do not carve them; they only know where they are hidden, and take them away as they need them. (*See Figure 35.*) I believe, though I am not certain of it, that they reserve the most interesting specimens for Dr. Cabrera: those that show scenes from the Superior Ancestors' everyday life, their inventions and their knowledge in all fields of science.

HUAQUEROS SELL STONES

There are few tourists in Ica and that is fortunate because *huaqueros,* now that they know the stones are very valuable, sometimes come to offer them for sale to residents of the Hotel Turista. How could an archaeologist resist such an offer?

We each bought half a dozen of them, showing birds, animals and people, but none of them was of any interest to the Primohistoric Library of Ica. They were more or less the same as the fifty stones we had seen in Professor Pezzia's museum.

I did not tell Dr. Cabrera about our escapade because its outcome surprised me so much, and also because I had no chance to talk with him, since our visit to Ocucaje took place just before our departure for Paracas.

Several points have been established: the stones are genuine, they are not carved in our time, and they come from ancient hiding places known only to *huaqueros*. About twenty thousand have been found so far, but Dr. Cabrera estimates that more than a hundred thousand still remain to be discovered. That figure does not seem exaggerated to me.

Actually, the engraved stones have been known for many years, probably since the seventeenth century,* but because most of them do not seem particularly surprising, they did not attract attention any more than ordinary flint tools or the pottery of Paracas.

Nearly all the Ica stones show relatively commonplace scenes. It was not until 1960 that Dr. Cabrera saw some truly revealing drawings: dinosaurs, giant termites and the first representations of human beings with prehistoric monsters. What was not obvious from two or three stones became so when scenes from the Mesozoic or Tertiary were repeated in ten or twenty engravings. Many archaeologists owned and handled stones from Ica, but only Dr. Cabrera gave meaning to the fantastic discovery.

THE WORLD WAS BORN AT ICA

In Peru the "Ica affair" has been passed over in almost total silence. Sometimes this seems to be the result of specific orders, but it is also possible that the

---

* In about 1958 Gregori B., restorer of the religion of the Inca Sun in Paris, showed me a paleotherium that ancient Mexicans or Pre-Incas had drawn from life, because the animal, a kind of tapir-rhinoceros of the Tertiary, wore a harness and stood among human beings.

Peruvians, by a strange kind of perversity, refuse to credit their country with the honor of being the First Land, the cradle of humanity.

"The world was born at Ica," proclaims Dr. Cabrera.

No one cares in Lima, from the presidential palace to the lowliest hovel.

And in France, from President Giscard d'Estaing to the most isolated shepherd, the same indifference is shown with regard to the marvelous site of Glozel. In Vichy, Clermont-Ferrand and Paris there are still people who stubbornly refuse to believe that the site is genuine. Confronted with conclusive evidence, they fiercely deny it.

In Ica there are also enemies of change, adversaries of anything that might alter the reassuring daily routine of people who are a little upset to see Monday give way to Tuesday, and Tuesday to Wednesday. According to them, Dr. Cabrera's stones were carved by shrewd Ocucaje peasants. "The more they make for him, the more he buys, and the more he buys, the older he thinks they are," they say with a knowing wink.

And because of unfounded gossip like that, a nation risks losing the privilege of being recognized as the seat of the world's oldest civilization and possessing the engraved stones that are the counterpart of the Lascaux cave paintings.

THE GLOZEL TACTIC

It is obvious that the revelations of the stones will revolutionize the study of history only insofar as it can be proved that they date from ancient times. And it is on this point that dishonesty, prejudices and passions will be unleashed.

As was to be expected, the Conspiracy has used its "Glozel tactic," which consists of slandering the collection without having seen it.

The marvelous black stones come from the vicinity

of Ica, where they are found in their natural state in the river valley. They look like stones that have been rolled by swift currents for a long time.

If the engravings are fraudulent—and this question must, of course, be raised—the counterfeiters are people from the region who used stones they found there. They are either crafty peasants or specialized workers employed by someone else: either Dr. Cabrera himself or a group of visionaries using this procedure to gain recognition for what they regard as the truth. In the latter case there would be no profit motive, which seems inadmissible to me, considering the great amount of labor that would have to be expended for such an uncertain result.

Just as I reject all suspicion with regard to Dr. Cabrera, I eliminate the possibility of dishonesty on the part of the peasants: they surely have enough manual skill to make the engravings, but not the knowledge that would be required. Their educational level would not enable them to imagine dinosaurs, continental drift and heart, kidney and brain transplants.

FRAUD IS IMPOSSIBLE

If an Ocucaje peasant had made the engravings by copying photographs or drawings supplied to him by someone else, he would have had to work more than thirty years in total secrecy!

In no part of the world is it possible for anyone to "fabricate" eleven thousand engraved stones, some of them quite large, without attracting the attention of people around him, or even the local authorities. Neither a peasant, nor specialized workers, nor Dr. Cabrera, nor visionary archaeologists could have escaped the watchful attention of neighbors made even more curious by the fact that almost nothing unusual ever happens in that out-of-the-way region of Peru.

Those eleven thousand engravings represent thirty

years of work at the rate of ten hours a day, not counting the time spent looking for stones, bringing them to the workshop, imagining the scenes to be drawn, sketching them and adjusting them to the sizes and shapes of the usable stones. Who would have devoted a major part of his life to a task that brought him no profit? Such a man would have been insane—a mad, admirable genius.

It was once thought that Emile Fradin was a mad genius in the "Glozel affair."

GLOZEL DATED AT TWENTY-NINE HUNDRED YEARS AGO: A MISTAKE

"I may be mad, but I'm not a genius," my friend Emile Fradin says sadly.

The inscribed tablets of Glozel are genuine, as has been proved by datings made in Denmark, Sweden and Norway, using the thermoluminescence method. The datings were carried out by Professors Arne Bjor and Vagn Mesdal of the Scientific Research Department of the Danish National Museum, Professor Lerje, head of the Atomic Research Laboratory at Risör, Norway, and Professor Silow of the Limhan Museum in Sweden.

The age of the tablets was said to be somewhere between twenty-seven hundred and twenty-nine hundred years. Establishing the authenticity of Glozel is important for the study of prehistory, but the datings announced by the Scandinavian scientists are not very satisfactory. Although the thermoluminescence method can attest to the antiquity of an object, it is not reliable for precise dating.

In my opinion the Glozel site goes back about seven thousand years. At that time reindeer, of which there are bones and drawings in Emile Fradin's museum, must have been still living in France, but their existence twenty-nine hundred years ago is rather doubtful.

A SALUTE TO DR. MORLET

What matters most here is not showing that Glozel goes back to the Magdalenian or the Neolithic, but proving conclusively that the French Prehistorical Society in 1926, a large group of pseudo-prehistorians and the enemies of the Fradin family, were maliciously dishonest or abysmally ignorant, or both.

The "great" prehistorians, such as Capitan, Breuil and Peyroni, were nothing but wreckers of the French archaeological heritage, unworthy of the high positions in which they had been rashly placed by politicians.

At this point I will salute, with affection and gratitude, those who took part in the struggle but died before they could have the reward and joy of seeing justice triumph: Claude and Antoine Fradin (Emile's grandfather and father), the valiant Dr. Antonin Morlet of Vichy, an intransigent champion of the cause, and the good Canon Léon Cote, a bold and witty defender of his Glozelian faith. (*See Figure 36.*)

Despite the mafia of official prehistorians and French national radio and television, the urns, tablets and engraved bones of Glozel have succeeded in asserting their authenticity. I am convinced that it will be the same with the Ica stones, if a method of dating can be applied to them. But it can already be stated categorically that they are genuine, since, as in the case of Glozel, fraud would be technically and materially impossible. At Glozel, Dr. Morlet caught Miss Garrod, Abbé Breuil's secretary, "in the act of falsification while the excavation committee was at work." It is not impossible that a few of the Ica stones may have been tampered with, but there is no justification for suspecting the vast majority of them. In the Louvre Museum many paintings are "attributed" to Titian, Perugino, Leonardo da Vinci or Raphael, but it would be unfair to conclude that the Louvre is a museum of fakes!

After examining some of the Ica stones, the mineralogist Mauricio Hochschild of Pisco, Peru, stated that both their incisions and their surfaces were covered in the same way by the natural oxidation that comes with age. Although he could not fix a precise date, he estimated that the engravings were at least several centuries old.

That is also the opinion of Colonel Omar Chioino Carranza, director of the Peruvian Aeronautical Museum, who has no doubt of the stones' authenticity.

"It seems certain," he told me, "that they're a message from a very ancient people whose memory has been lost by history. They were engraved several thousand years ago. They've been known in Peru for a long time, and my museum has more than four hundred of them."

PRESERVATION OF THE ENGRAVINGS

If the views of prehistorians and paleontologists were correct, these stones would be at least sixty million years old, dating from the time when the dinosaurs died out. But prehistorians and paleontologists are mistaken.

They recognize it to some extent, since they admit that in certain parts of the world, *particularly in America,* the reign of the dinosaurs continued till a much more recent time than is generally believed. Drawings of dinosaurs have been found on rocks in the Amazon Valley.

Twenty miles from Baku, in the Soviet Union, stands a rock carved in the shape of a dinosaur. After eliminating the possibility that it might have been shaped by natural erosion, geologists now believe it is a human work dating from about ten thousand years ago—fifty million years after the supposed disappearance of the species depicted!

The existence of the last dinosaurs has finally been situated at the beginning of the Quaternary. Can engraved stones be preserved that long?

Thousands of engraved stones are stored in Dr. Cabrera's secret sanctuary at Ica.

This man is unquestionably examining a drawing through a magnifying glass.

Photo Kuroki

Men examining rock carvings, or perhaps fossils, through a magnifying glass.

Photo Kuroki

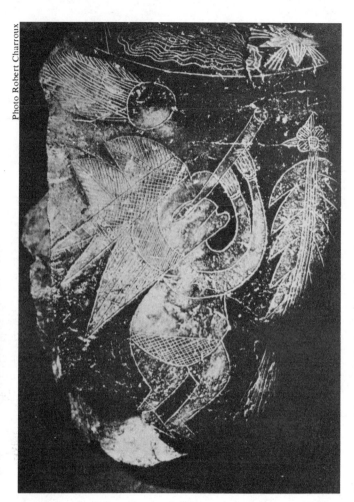

Photo Robert Charroux

Astronomer looking at the sky through a telescope.

Like the aluminum plaque placed aboard the American spacecraft Pioneer 10 in 1972, the cosmography at the top of the drawing may be intended to locate the cosmic homeland of the extraterrestrial Intelligences who designed it.

For the time being, that cosmography is impenetrable. Perhaps it is related to a past comet that dated the arrival of Superior Ancestors on Earth, or to a future comet that will mark their return or apocalyptic events.

The top of the Astronomers' Stone is a jigsaw puzzle of cosmography and geography, with stars, comets, continents, seas—and a boat that evokes the great Deluge.

Photo Kuroki

A map from the Mesozoic era?

Here is Dr. Cabrera's interpretation:

A: Land of Mu; B: North America; C: South America; D: Atlantis.

Another geographic representation:

E: Europe; F: Africa; G: Asia-Lemuria; H: Australia.

The "rivers" flowing through the oceans may be either intercontinental sealanes or ocean currents.

By turning the map, one can see that each continent has the form of a human face.

Another hypothesis: these drawings represent the hemispheres of the home planet of the extraterrestrial Intelligences of Ica. If so, the sky observed by the astronomers in other drawings may indicate the region of the cosmos where the planet is located.

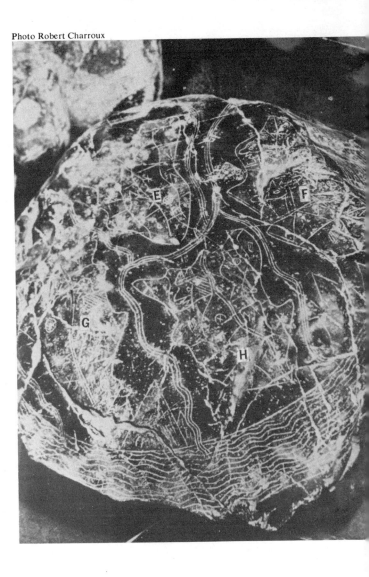

Two men attacking a dinosaur, one with an axe, the other with a knife. A primate servant falls, wounded by the monster, perhaps a brachiosaur, the heaviest of the dinosaurs (fifty tons, eighty feet long), which lived a hundred and forty million years ago.

At the bottom, on the left-hand stone, is an animal that might be an amphibian, the dendrerpeton (ten inches long).

On the lower right-hand stone is one of the first birds, the archaeopteryx. It was the size of a crow and lived a hundred and eighty million years ago.

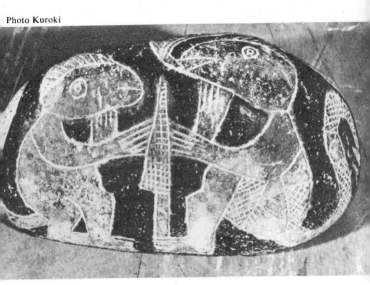

Primates of Ica, half human and half saurian.

Dr. Cabrera in his museum. To his right is a portrait of his ancestor Jeronimo, founder of the city of Ica.
    Lower left: the cesarean stone.

Cesarean operation, first phase. The surgeon palpates the patient as she lies on a bed. The baby, in his mother's womb, is naked. We see the knife that will be used for the operation: it is made of metal, with a blade attached to the handle by three rivets.

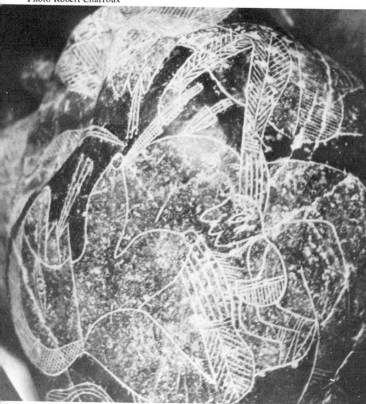

Cesarean operation, second phase. The woman, with a strongly aquiline nose, is lying naked. In front of her, the surgeon operates according to the standard technique, but in the time-continuum peculiar to the Mayas and Incas: the past and the future are mingled in the present. Thus the surgeon is preparing to open the patient's womb with a knife held in his right hand, while with his left hand he seems to be already drawing out the baby, who is now wearing a diaper. Skeptics have used this detail in maintaining that the artist lived in the sixteenth century and had been conditioned by Christianity to regard nakedness as a sin.

Note the breath coming from the woman's mouth, indicating that she is alive.

Cesarean operation, third phase. A kind of demon, or a strange half-man, half-stegosaur creature, is taking part in the delivery. He is not a primate like the one shown in the scene depicting an attack on a dinosaur. He wears a loincloth, which gives him a certain human character, but on his back are "fins" like those of a stegosaur.

In the patient's mouth is a tube with a bulb at its other end. Is it for the purpose of supplying her with oxygen or some sort of liquid? In any case it is a device for contributing to the success of the operation.

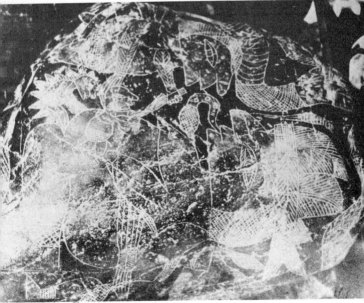

Photo Robert Charroux

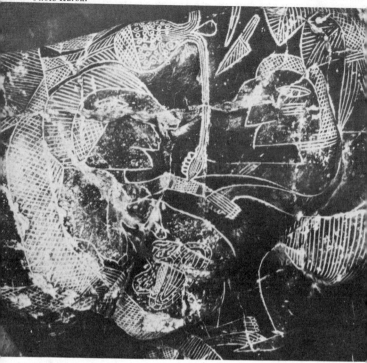

TAKING BLOOD

The surgeon, on the right, holds a pump by which he takes blood from a woman who is pregnant, judging from her large breasts and swollen nipples. The phenomenon of rejection will be avoided by means of this particular blood.

The woman's wrist is bandaged, the needle attached to the pump is plunged into her radial vein, and the blood goes through a flexible tube to the container in which it is collected.

The blood is depicted in a scientific way, I believe, if the sinuous figures in the vase represent the blood plasma and if the circular figures represent the red corpuscles.

The woman is lying on a kind of bed. The photograph should be turned so that this bed is horizontal, which will show that the surgeon is raising the patient's arm to make the blood flow through the tube and into the vase. It will then be seen that the vase rests on a support, which in turn rests on the edge of the bed. The scene thus takes on its logical meaning. Only the surgeon is placed in an abnormal position, necessitated by the narrowness of the andesite stone.

As if he were gifted with double sight—and perhaps he was—the artist has depicted the woman's abdominal viscera.

OPERATION ON THE DONOR

The donor is on an operating table. The surgeon touches the heart he is about to remove, while his assistant holds a container of surgical instruments.

REMOVAL OF THE HEART

The surgeon has taken out the heart, still connected to the body by the aorta.

At the top of the drawing are the assistant's hands, holding instruments.

PREPARATION OF THE ORGAN

The heart is completely removed. A device has been attached to its blood vessels, either a stopper or an irrigation apparatus (between the base of the organ and the container).

The surgeon is engaged in a cleaning procedure. He has a whole array of bistouries at his disposal.

Photo Robert Charroux

BLOOD TRANSFUSION

The recipient, lying on the operating table, suffers from myocarditis, with a lesion of the heart indicated by an oval with lines drawn across it. To prepare him for the operation and avoid rejection, he is being given a transfusion of blood taken from the pregnant woman. The surgeon is inserting a needle into a vein in the right wrist, which has been bandaged.

As in the preceding drawings, the artist has depicted the patient's heart, esophagus, stomach and intestines.

The recipient is breathing (air is shown coming from his mouth), which may mean that he has not been anesthetized.

IRRIGATION OF THE HEART

The donor's heart is irrigated with blood from the pregnant woman. A blood-extracting apparatus (near the surgeon's knee) is shown connected with the patient's aortic system; this blood will be used in the following phases for irrigating the donor's heart and keeping it alive.

No breath is shown coming from the woman's mouth; she has probably been anesthetized.

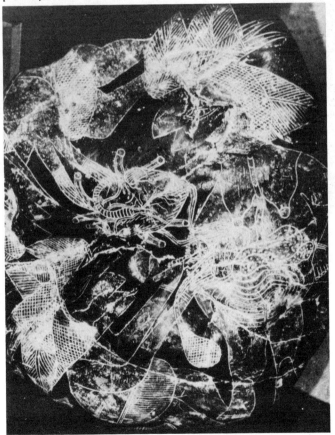

Photo Robert Charroux

FIRST PHASE OF THE TRANSPLANT

The surgeon incises the abdomen, the first phase of the operation.

It seems that in all the drawings, perhaps because of space limitations, the artist made the thorax coincide with the abdomen. This shows that he was not a surgeon, but was only reporting what he had seen.

I believe that the heart surgeons had enough scientific knowledge to enable them to practice anesthesia, perhaps with plants.

*REMOVAL OF THE RECIPIENT'S SICK HEART, WITH
ITS ARTERIOVENOUS VESSELS*
*Notice that under the operating table a leaf is drawn with its stem
in the direction of the patient's head, a sign that, with this orientation, indicates that he is alive.*

Photo Robert Charroux

The surgeon holds the donor's heart, which is connected to a per-fusion system that performs the function of the heart and lungs in sustaining the irrigated organ.

The recipient apparently remains a certain time without a heart. It is likely that other stones, not yet found, explain how he can stay alive, perhaps by means of anticoagulants or an artificial slowing of the organic functions.

INSERTION OF THE HEALTHY HEART INTO THE THORAX
The organ is connected to a device that nourishes it with blood taken from the pregnant woman.

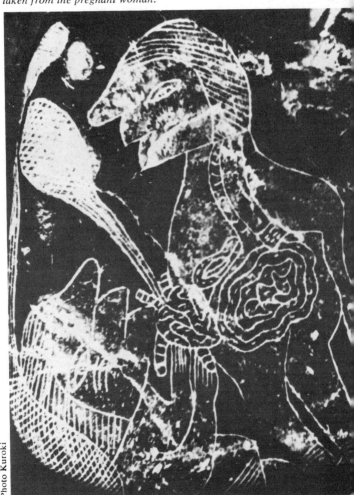

Photo Kuroki

THE HEART IS PUT IN PLACE

It is still irrigated by perfusion.

Below, on the same stone, is an indication of the first phase of the transplant: incision of the abdomen.

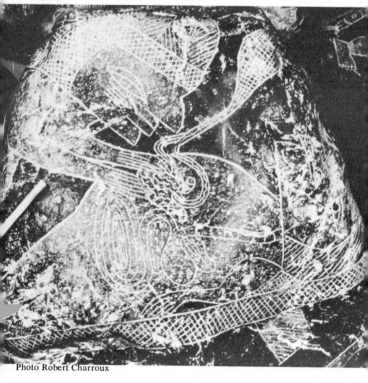

Photo Robert Charroux

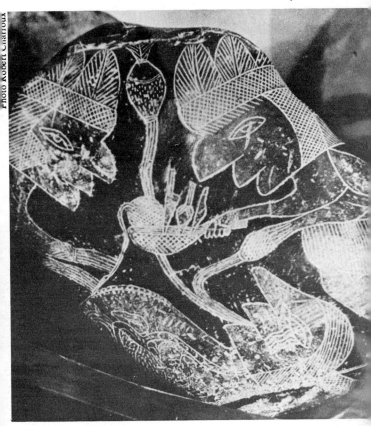

THE TRANSPLANT IS FINISHED

The surgeon sews up the abdominal wall and the thorax with a needle and thread. With one hand, his assistant holds a container of instruments. With his other hand, he squeezes a bulb that forces in a gas, probably air or oxygen. Another device introduces a liquid into the patient's mouth.

Whatever the exact purpose of the procedure, it was obviously drawn by someone who had often witnessed advanced surgical operations, even if he was unable to perform them himself, and even if he made mistakes in depicting them.

POSTOPERATIVE CARE

The operation has succeeded, judging from the symbolic leaf under the table. (Its stem is pointed in the opposite direction when death is present. This symbolism appears on many of the Ica stones.)

The surgeon is checking the heart with a stethoscope. In his hands he holds the needle and thread.

The stethoscope (at first made of wood) was supposedly invented by the French physician Laënnec in about 1800. The instrument shown on the stones is thousands of years older and seems to have rubber tubes.

LAST PHASE OF THE OPERATION

The surgeon is probably about to disconnect the device introducing a liquid into the patient's mouth.

Everything leads us to believe that the operation had a satisfactory outcome.

Photo Robert Charroux

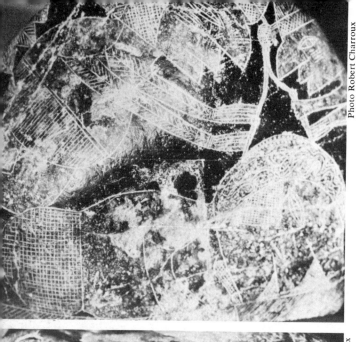

Photo Robert Charroux

Photo Robert Charroux

Opposite page, top: Two surgeons working on the scalp with the strange instrument we saw in the heart transplant, but in this case it has two jointed branches which may be mechanized sewing devices, judging from the areas with white dots in them. Opposite page, bottom: The patient is lying on a bed or an operating table. His skull is shaved and the surgeon is apparently making an incision with a bistoury. Behind him, a convoluted mass suggests that an excision has been performed.

In contrast to the two pictures of a brain transplant, we here see two surgeons extracting snakes from the skull of a patient who is probably "possessed" or insane.

The belief that certain illnesses were caused by such things as worms, snakes or stones may not have been entirely groundless: it is possible that, as knowledge was distorted in the process of being handed down from generation to generation, viruses came to be regarded as dangerous worms or snakes, and gallstones were identified with ordinary stones. But it is strange that superstition concerning snakes was able to coexist with a science far enough advanced to achieve organ transplants.

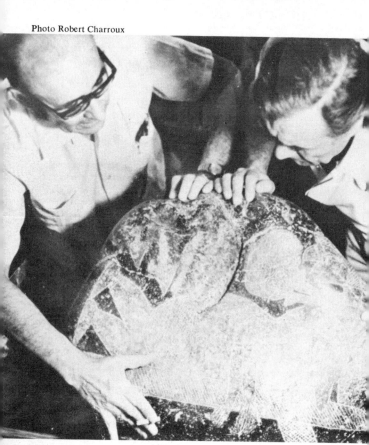

Dr. Cabrera and Francis Mazière examine a large stone depicting a brain transplant.

A poor village in the desert: Ocucaje, which will soon be famous.

Ducks' nest among the engraved stones stored in an Ocucaje peasant's farmyard.

The clay tablets of "Ashurbanipal's Library" (Nineveh, Assyria) are in a perfect state of preservation, but they are only 2,640 years old.

Pieces of limestone with drawings on them, found at Lussac-les-Châteaux, France, date from about twenty thousand years ago and are slightly calcified. They are generally recognized as the oldest known stone documents.

The andesite of Ica is harder than the clay of Nineveh but softer than the limestone of Lussac. It is difficult to give an authoritative opinion, but it does not seem that an engraving in limestone could last a hundred thousand years; it would probably be effaced long before that time.

There is thus one mystery concerning the preservation of the Ica engravings and another concerning their presence in a region where, even in the time of the Incas, civilization was only a reflection of the great neighboring centers: Cuzco, Arequipa, Pachacamac, Chavin, etc. There was, of course, a Nasca culture, and it was among the most brilliant, but it goes back only two thousand years, which places it far from the end of the dinosaurs.

The early Ica engravers certainly saw dinosaurs, and the later engravers were contemporaries of societies or Initiators who had great scientific knowledge. This apparent incompatibility is resolved in the light of discoveries recently made by avant-garde archaeologists, not only in South America but on all the continents.

UNKNOWN PYRAMIDS AND
FLYING CYLINDERS IN CHINA

In Swaziland, Africa, the anthropologist Adrian Boshier and the geologist Peter Beaumont, both Australian, excavated an ancient hematite mine that, according to their dating tests, had been exploited 43,224 years ago.

Science writer Jacques Bergier reports that in Siberia a Soviet scientist named Alexander Kazantzev exhumed the skeleton of a bison whose skull had been penetrated by a *bullet* forty thousand years ago.

"Who could have used firearms at that time?" wonders Bergier.

Chinese archaeologists, including Professor Chi Penlao of the University of Peking, have recognized several pyramids, nearly a thousand feet high, that were submerged in Lake Tungfling, Yunnan Province, as the result of an earthquake. Their submersion took place more than three thousand years ago, but their age has not yet been determined.

On an island in the same lake, and in the granitic mountains around it, extraordinary drawings were engraved forty-five thousand years ago. They represent people carrying large horn-shaped objects that are presumed to be weapons. Flying above them are mysterious cylinders whose passengers are people with smaller horn-shaped weapons. (This account appeared in the German magazine *Der Bund* and was reported by the French magazine *Ouranos* in October 1973.)

TELESCOPES THIRTY THOUSAND YEARS AGO

The telescope was known in very ancient times.

It was described in the thirteenth century by Roger Bacon, and by the German Jesuit Athanasius Kircher about 1650.

The British Museum has a glass lens four thousand years old, found in the ruins of Nineveh. A gigantic glass plaque was discovered in Palestine, and concave mirrors that may have been parts of optical instruments have been found in South America, North Africa and Iraq.

Aristotle reports that the ancients looked at the heavenly bodies "through long tubes." Euclid (third century B.C.) formulated rules for making eyeglasses, and Strabo, at the beginning of the Christian era, knew the telescope. According to Jean de Kerdeland (*Télé-7 Jours,* No. 750), when Caesar was planning to invade Britain, he observed its coast from France.

There is a reference to the telescope in the *Shu-Ching,* the most famous ancient Chinese historical work: "The successor of Emperor Yao [died 2258 B.C.] went into the Room of the Ancestors, where the heavenly bodies are depicted, and there he saw the tube with which they were observed."

Professor Michanowsky, an astronomer, categorically states that the ancestors of the Incas had astronomical observatories and telscopes comparable to ours in every way.

NASA astronomers think that people in ancient times, about thirty thousand years ago, observed explosions of novae invisible to the naked eye.

In 1956 Professor Michanowsky discovered in Bolivia a stone covered with astronomical signs. When he studied the engravings he was amazed to find that they represented a region of the sky where a supernova had exploded thirty thousand years ago, giving birth to the Gum nebula.

In obvious correlation with this discovery, he learned that each year, at the exact place where he had found the stone, the Indians had a ritual gathering to commemorate an event that none of them could identify. Furthermore a legend stated that the part of the sky occupied by the nebula was called "the region of the celestial ostrich hunt."

"Long ago," said the Indians, "the celestial ostrich was chased across the sky by two dogs. They caught it and ate it."

This story clearly evokes the ancient time during which a great cosmic cataclysm brought terror to the people of the Andes.

Michanowsky found that from the site of the stone and the rite it was impossible to see the Gum nebula with the naked eye. This led him to conclude that the explosion of the nebula could only have been seen with the aid of a telescope. He is now looking for places where observatories may have been built.

His view is supported by rock paintings discovered in California, depicting the explosion of the supernova that became the Crab nebula. They were found in 1964 by Muriel Kennedy and authenticated as an astronomical representation by Stephen Maran of the Goddard Space Flight Center. Robert Harrington, an astronomer at the Washington Naval Observatory, calculated to within one degree the position of the moon shown in the paintings, in relation to the Crab nebula, and fixed the date of observation at July 5, 1054.

Thus the Ancestors whose existence is denied by the Conspiracy developed highly scientific civilizations not only in the ancient empire of the Incas, but also in North America, and no doubt in other places as well.

In view of this, it becomes easier to accept the idea that the people of ancient Ica used telescopes and had medical and technical knowledge that has been familiar to us for only a century.

Professor Michanowsky's Pre-Inca American Indians seem to authenticate Dr. Cabrera's engraved stones and give an indication of their age: thirty thousand years.

INITIATORS WHO CAME FROM THE SKY ELEVEN THOUSAND YEARS AGO

We can now feel more at ease in asserting the authenticity of the Superior Ancestors and the Ica stones.

In the time span between eleven and thirty thousand years ago—from the observation of the Gum nebula to several centuries after the Deluge—it is possible to assume preservation of the engravings and coexistence of dinosaurs and human beings with great scientific knowledge.

If the stones were engraved at Ica, an important question still remains to be answered: how were dinosaurs, even in small numbers, able to live in a region where stony deserts are much more numerous than green valleys? Most dinosaurs were herbivores and each of them consumed at least a ton of greenery every day. They lived in marshy areas where abundant water enabled plant life to be luxuriant. Since Ica does not fit this description, I am inclined to think that either the stones were not engraved there or the climate of Peru has changed to an extent that is hard to accept within a period of only thirty thousand years.

The material of the stones is typical of the Ica region. The least dubious specimens show that the engravers did not perform surgical operations themselves and that the library was created on the basis of documents, copies or instructions given by Initiators. This is only a hypothesis, but it seems to me the one best suited to providing an explanation in an area where conventional reasoning is ineffective.

In the same order of ideas, we can say that the Ica stones date from post-Deluge times when Initiators who were called gods and necessarily came "from the sky," since no known civilization existed on Earth then, stimulated the development of civilizations in Egypt, Peru, Tiahuanaco and the lands of the Celts.

It appears that there was an incursion of extraterrestrial Initiators shortly after each of the two historical deluges: twelve thousand and five thousand years ago, respectively. Some of those Initiators left records on the basis of which Pre-Inca artists engraved the first of the Ica stones about eleven thousand years ago. The work was continued by a chain of Initiates until about the sixteenth century A.D. This hypothesis meets the objections that can be raised and fits the data we possess.

The extraterrestrial Initiators were able to perform

heart transplants and they had also acquired the knowledge needed for reproducing prehistoric animal species, either from their studies or from having visited Earth in the time of the dinosaurs. Before they went back to their home planet or were absorbed into the mass of ignorant earthlings, they or their deteriorated descendants left a testimony to their knowledge. (*See Figure 37.*)

A MESSAGE FROM THE ATLANTEANS?

Another hypothesis, equally attractive, has the further advantage of being in accord with traditional data.

Before the great Deluge that occurred twelve thousand years ago, our Superior Ancestors the Atlanteans (or perhaps the inhabitants of the Land of Mu) developed an earthly civilization of which ours is only a reflection.

Twelve thousand years ago Initiates knew that the earthly intelligentsia was going to be totally destroyed by a great cataclysm. All mythologies agree that some Initiates knew about the Deluge in advance: Noah, Manu in India, Bochica in Colombia, Xisuthros in Chaldea, Coxcox in Mexico, etc.

Esotericists maintain that these Initiates took the precaution of recording the essence of their knowledge so that the secret would not be lost with them. These archives of our Superior Ancestors were never found—until the discovery of Dr. Cabrera's Primohistoric Library.

According to this hypothesis, the Ica stones present the main outlines of the *useful* knowledge that the Atlanteans wanted to convey to us. Deliberately unrecorded were certain techniques that might lead to development of the atomic bomb and other destructive devices. This would explain the taboo on the wheel among the peoples of the Andes.

These archives could not be recorded on such perishable materials as wood, paper or metal. It is also reasonable to assume that the Initiates used the services of ordinary craftsmen skilled in engraving in order to make the records more understandable to peoples at a lower stage of development. The choice of material and workers, and the fact that the same task was carried out in several workshops in different parts of the world, would explain the archaic and schematic nature of the scenes depicted. Unless—and this possibility deserves consideration—the engravings were made *after* the Deluge, from memory and on the basis of incomplete documents, by Atlantean survivors belonging to the less intellectual classes of society.

The stones were stored in dry places at average altitude, where it was likely that they would be discovered someday. The Ica deposit is not the only one that still exists (traditions speak of consecrated places in Tibet, Egypt and India). Another one has been found at Acambaro, Mexico.

HIGHLY INTELLIGENT ENGRAVERS

I freely admit that my theories are not scientifically rigorous and are open to dispute. One objection, in particular, disturbs me: some of the drawings have a sharpness, precision and sureness that arouse suspicion!

The man who engraved the heart operation was obviously highly intelligent—an artist, geometer and mathematician with the mental structures to calculate, project his thought and synthesize. His intelligence must have been as keen as that of Leonardo da Vinci, and his manual dexterity as great as that of an architect, a surgeon or a cartoonist.

My conviction is based on the sureness of the line, which in each drawing begins at the top of the surgeon's headdress and sometimes draws the forehead, nose, mouth and chin in a single movement. The rest of the drawing is in the same vein: the curves seem to have been done with a compass and the straight lines could not be straighter if they had been drawn with a ruler.

The synthesis of the lines in the drawing representing a small horse or an onager (*see Figure 38*) could have come only from a mind much more highly developed than that of the average person living today.

How were those pure, rigorous lines drawn? With obsidian or a metal tool?

To form my own opinion, I took some stones of the same hardness and tried to copy some of the drawings, using an electric engraving tool that easily cuts into limestone and is held like a pencil.

I hoped I could do as well as the prehistoric engravers but my skill was unequal to the task and the result was disappointing. It did, however, establish one thing quite clearly: the drawings on the Ica stones were not done in our time with an electric tool!

But I had already known that.

FIVE FINGERS OF EQUAL LENGTH

There are many representations of human beings on the stones. They are of various types, though most have an Incan profile and wear a feathered headdress and a loincloth. They have one interesting feature: each hand has five fingers of the same length; that is, they have no thumbs.

According to Andes traditions reported by Gregori B., also known as Garcia Beltran, restorer of the religion of the Inca Sun, the mother of mankind was named Orejona. Long ago she came to Earth in a spacecraft brighter than the sun and landed on the shore of Lake Titicaca. Like the personages carved on the Gate of the Sun of Tiahuanaco, she had only four fingers on each hand, including a thumb. The men on the Ica stones therefore do not seem to belong to the same race as the legendary mother of mankind.

The general law of the irreversibility of evolution expressly states (but is it accurate?) that there is no return after a specialization. It follows that we may be descended from ancestors with five or six fingers, but not four.

The more fingers a hand has, the more primitive it is. It would seem, then, that the hands of the men on the Ica stones are not those of Superior Ancestors, but of native earthlings who made reproductions, with their own physical characteristics, of scenes, events and surgical operations whose protagonists were more highly advanced beings from another planet.

Nevertheless, despite the statements of biologists, I believe that the presumed inhabitants of other planets may have reached a very high stage of civilization and become differentiated from us in minor ways.

ICA, LUSSAC-LES-CHÂTEAUX AND LASCAUX

I have studied the various prehistoric techniques of painting and drawing, either at the sites themselves or in original documents. In 1947 I was able to see and photograph the cave paintings of Montignac-Lascaux, I know Altamira very well, and I live within a few miles of Lussac-les-Châteaux, where in 1937 my friend Léon Péricard discovered the priceless Magdalenian Library (fifteen to twenty thousand years old). I am also lucky enough to own an engraved stone from Lussac and thirteen from Ica, and some inscribed pottery from Glozel, given to me by my friend Emile Fradin, not to mention several other pieces from Easter Island, San Agustin, Peru, Egypt, etc.

We must become used to this idea: judging from these engravings and objects, our prehistoric ancestors had much surer hands than ours, and an understanding of lines that would force a graphologist to conclude that they had highly developed intellectual faculties. The engraved personages of Lussac and the "marvelous horse" of Lascaux, to take only two examples, give evidence of a skill equal to that of the Ica engravers.

Moreover, we must bear in mind that the Indians of Mexico and Peru have innate artistic abilities that are unequaled anywhere else in the world. Someday the so-called civilized peoples will realize that Mexican painters are far superior to those of Europe and that the Incas of Peru have mathematical minds better conditioned than Einstein's.

This was recently pointed out by Professor Otto Klineberg of Columbia University, with regard to the Indians of North America. The case of the Hopis is especially remarkable. Since World War II a number of them have been going to college and it has been noted that they feel amazingly at ease in mathematics and theoretical physics. Anthropologists studied the phenomenon and discovered that the Hopi language seemed to have been specially designed for expressing the most abstract concepts of relativistic physics. Before the development of that physics, Hopi logic seemed absurd to Europeans. The Hopis were retarded because they were too advanced.

The mental processes of "primitive" peoples must be taken into consideration if we want to try to understand their art and the documents they have left us.

BEHEADING FOR ADULTERY

Aside from the virtuosity of the engravers, which appears in different degrees, there is not much unity in the Ica stones. They reveal several styles, techniques and varieties of patina that show they were done by a number of different engravers.

For example, the stone showing a knife duel has an engraving and a patina more recent than the ones showing dinosaurs, which do not have the fluidity of line found in the depiction of surgical operations. It seems that the different engravings were made thousands of years apart.

Countless engravings deal with zoology or scenes apparently without interest, but there is never any representation of agriculture, crafts or industry. There are, however, engravings that convey legal principles whose interpretation leaves little room for doubt: sexual relations were forbidden between brothers and sisters unless they were of royal blood (as with the ancient Egyptians and Incas); an adulterous woman was beheaded, while punishment of the guilty man was limited to having his penis cut off; like his mother, the child of an adulterous union was beheaded.

But if the Ica stones are pages of a "book of world history," and if the Superior Ancestors were able to perform heart transplants, how are we to explain certain disconcerting lacks? Except for boats carrying Indians who strongly resemble Incas, no means of locomotion are shown. Nor are there any cities, parks, books or heating devices. Houses are shown only rarely.

And there is nothing with wheels or gears. This supports the view of those who relate the Ica stones to Andes civilization. No compasses, no containers that give the impression of being made of glass—which is quite surprising for a people who had telescopes and magnifying glasses!

"I can't guarantee that the civilization of ancient Ica had no inventions," says Dr. Cabrera, "but on the eleven thousand stones I own, and the twenty thousand that are estimated to be scattered among other collectors, no drawings of cars, airplanes or rockets have ever been found. A large number of stones are still missing, however. They're in a place known to my friends the peasants."

ENGRAVINGS FOR WHOM?

One argument used against the authenticity of the Ica stones is the incongruity between the advanced technology shown in the engravings and the way the personages are dressed.

"Is it plausible," say the critics, "that men performing an operation as sophisticated as a heart transplant would be wearing only loincloths?"

The argument has a certain weight, and it forces us to believe, as I have already said, that the people who made the engravings were not the same as those who performed the operations. What matters is to know *who* wanted to transmit that knowledge and *how* they decided to transmit it.

The Superior Ancestors certainly wanted to leave a record of their existence and teachings to accelerate the development of future societies. We must imagine them as scientists in a time when all other peoples (native earthlings, on my supposition) were in a half-savage state, and perhaps still living with the last of the dinosaurs. Would they record their knowledge on film or paper? No, they knew that such materials would last only a few centuries, so they used the almost indestructible materials of the primitive people around them: stone and ceramics.

And it would have been pointless for them to give precise, detailed descriptions of what they were capable of doing. Suppose they had left a photographically realistic engraving of an operation. What would it have meant to primitive people? They would have seen it only as a picture of men in white gowns standing around an altar covered with white cloth.

The Ica engravings do not give detailed instructions

for performing a heart transplant or making a telescope, but they do indicate that it is *possible* to transplant a heart and look at the stars through a magnifying instrument.

If the engravings date from eleven thousand years ago, what kind of clothes should the people depicted in them have been wearing? Should they have been shown in sixteenth-century jerkins in case the engravings were discovered by the conquistadores? In stovepipe hats for nineteenth-century discoverers? In blue jeans for our own time? Since the time of discovery was uncertain, it would have been foolish to give the engravings a style and an amount of detail that might have made them incomprehensible to their discoverers.

Their design is remarkably intelligent on the assumption that the Superior Ancestors—extraterrestrials, Atlanteans, Muians, or others—deliberately had ignorant people transcribe messages intended for other more or less ignorant people.

THE INITIATORS WERE CLAIRVOYANT

All those conflicting, incomprehensible and anachronistic ideas and scenes are enough to disturb our usual ways of thinking. But there is another mystery, known only to Dr. Cabrera and me, presented by certain stones whose existence will probably remain unknown to the general public for a long time.

Although I am not authorized to reveal that mystery, I can say that the Ica stones tell about events that took place long before the time of the dinosaurs. Furthermore they describe major events in the human adventure that neither the engravers nor the Superior Ancestors could have known from personal experience, for they took place *thousands of years after the engravings were made.*

I cannot say more on the subject, beyond adding this statement: either the engravers of the Ica stones were clairvoyant or they did their work on the basis of instructions from Superior Ancestors who were both scientists and clairvoyant.

Perhaps they acted under the influence of hallucinogenic drugs. That would have been perfectly in keeping with ancient art: the paintings, sculpture and drawings of the Indians (at Ellora, Ajanta, Madurai, etc.), the ancient Mexicans and the Incas are masterpieces conceived under the influence of hashish, coca or hallucinogenic mushrooms.

We must, however, consider another hypothesis, one that would eliminate clairvoyance from this mystery: the hypothesis that the engravings depicting events that took place in the last two thousand years were made after the Spanish conquest about four hundred years ago.

This explanation would be in agreement with esoteric writings. It assumes that until fairly recent times there was a succession of unknown Initiates, repositories of tradition and remote history, in sanctuaries that existed in America and may still exist in the Far East.

On this theory, the Rosicrucian Order is much older than is commonly thought; its origin goes back to extremely ancient times and the significant facts of human history are recorded by a chain of Knowers living in sanctuaries that are either under the surface of our planet or outside our universe. Revelations like the Ica stones are communciated to us in an esoteric way in order to preserve the mystery of the sanctuaries and the Knowers.

Finally, another hypothesis can be proposed: the Ica stones are a legacy from members of a superior human race for whom time does not have the same meaning as for us, and who therefore have simultaneous knowledge of the past, present and future.

THERE ARE OTHER HIDING PLACES

Although these speculations are often hazardous and sometimes contrary to Dr. Cabrera's views, they enable us to assemble a few pieces of the puzzle:

1. The stones are genuine and have been found in Peru for a long time.

2. They are engraved in the style of prehistoric peoples, witness Lascaux, Lussac, San Agustin, Glozel.

3. They cannot have been preserved intact more than forty thousand years and hence were not contemporaneous with dinosaurs, even if the latter were still living at the beginning of the Pleistocene, one million years ago.

4. They were engraved by a people less advanced than we are, but in accordance with orders or documents from Superior Ancestors who had probably disappeared before the time when the engraving was done.

5. They summarize the useful knowledge that the Superior Ancestors wanted to transmit to peoples who had survived the Deluge or an unknown cataclysm.

6. There must be other deposits of the same kind, in other places.

7. The Superior Ancestors were either Atlanteans from before the Deluge or extraterrestrial Initiators whose ancestors had visited Earth in earlier geological eras, or who knew those eras through scientific study.

8. An initiatory chain has been perpetuated through the ages and revelations come to us at fixed dates by order of the Knowers, although we believe they come from fortuitous discoveries.

This balance sheet is positive, even though it only points up the mystery, but another prodigious discovery, made in Mexico, adds valuable support to the authenticity of the Ica stones.

For there really are other hiding places.

CHAPTER 5

The Thirty-Two Thousand
Messages of Acambaro

THE PRIMOHISTORIC LIBRARY of Ica is not the only
one of its kind, since even in France there is the Prehistoric Library of Lussac-les-Châteaux, which is almost equally significant, although it goes back no
farther than the Magdalenian period, fifteen to twenty
thousand years ago.* These stone books, which, like
those of Dr. Cabrera, tell a story totally different from
the legends invented by prehistorians, were for a long
time (beginning in 1935) sequestered in the Museum

* The Magdalenian, the period of Lascaux, Altamira and Lussac-
les-Châteaux, is said to have been at the end of what prehistorians call
the most recent ice age. It is also called the "reindeer age" because
reindeer lived in France at that time—just as they now live in French
national parks! We now know that animals from prehistoric or ancient
times continued living until relatively recent periods in areas that were
favorable to them and not particularly cold—at Glozel, for example.

81

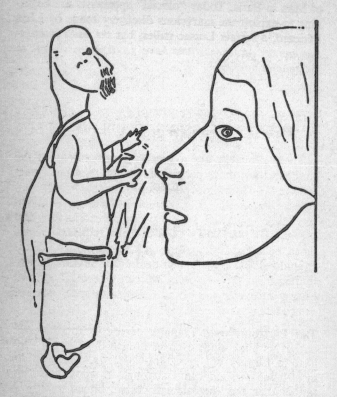

Left: This bald, bearded Magdalenian man, apparently wearing slippers and a dressing gown, looks more like a philosopher or an orator than a club-wielding brute incapable of imagining and building a wall.

Right: The "Young Lady of Lussac," with her neatly combed hair and delicate features, also bears no resemblance to the brutes invented by official pundits. Yet she was born twenty thousand years before Brigitte Bardot. "Prehistorians" are frauds. (Drawings by Stéphane Lwoff.)

of Man in Paris. Today "official" specialists are beginning to exploit the marvelous discovery made by Léon Péricard, a former Lussac miller, but *the most interesting human representations have never been shown to the general public.*

THE WELL-DRESSED PEOPLE OF TWENTY THOUSAND YEARS AGO

These drawings are a great embarrassment to the pundits: they show people of twenty thousand years ago dressed more or less the same as people today!

Since they supposedly lived in an "ice age," it might be assumed that they were warmly dressed in furs. But not at all: they wore hats, jackets, trousers, socks, shoes, belts and robes. And since the men often walked around half naked with their penises ostentatiously protruding from their trousers, we can take the liberty of having serious doubts about the polar climate decreed by academic authorities!

Some of them had carefully combed hair, others had "crew cuts," and some wore mustaches and goatees, all of which shows an esthetic concern that is hard to reconcile with the conventional view of them as savage cave-dwellers, half human and half animal, who gorged themselves on raw meat and were incapable of building a hut or forging an axe.

This is a rather strange way to consider people who were skilled chemists (the sticks of iron peroxide and manganese peroxide at Lascaux), learned astronomers (they had lunar calendars thirty thousand years ago), engravers of symbols three hundred thousand years ago (the bone discovered by the prehistorian Bordes), tailors, weavers, barbers, jewelers, shoemakers, hairdressers, surgeons, etc.

La Marche cave—Magdalenian III—Lussac-leś-Châ-teaux, France.

This woman lived two hundred centuries ago, in the time of the Lascaux cave paintings, mammoths and chipped flint tools. She is dressed in the manner of our own time. Here is what the prehistorian Lwoff has written about her: "With what looks to us like a sailor's waterproof hat on her head, this woman is completely dressed. . . . There appears to be a pocket on the right leg of her trousers, over her thigh. . . . A sole is clearly visible under her foot." (Drawing by Stéphane Lwoff.)

THE MESSAGES OF ACAMBARO

A PREHISTORIAN WHO KNOWS THE ROPES

The history of ancient peoples is almost totally unknown. Conventional prehistorians have determined the names and classifications of cultures and civilizations, and in spite of proofs and discoveries, everything that does not fit into the sacrosanct categories is said to be either whimsical or nonexistent.

Recognition was withheld from Glozel for a long time, and it is still withheld from Atlantis, Mu, the Masma culture discovered by my friend Daniel Ruzo, Petra, Zimbabwe, the civilization of vitrified forts in France and Great Britain, and the incredible Mexican civilization of Acambaro. Incredible, yes, because, like Dr. Cabrera's stones, the figurines found at Acambaro invalidate many conventional theories and revolutionize zoology and paleontology.

The remarkable American science writer Alexander Marshack has demonstrated the errors of anthropologists and the scandalous negligence of French museums. He shows that prehistoric people had reached a much higher level of thought than is taught in France. They calculated, conjectured, estimated, made calendars; in short, their minds worked exactly as ours do. Marshack's discovery is also revolutionary, and it has not been received without ill-humor.

In an interview conducted by Fanny Deschamps and published in the French magazine *Elle* in 1973, Marshack tells of his frustrating experience with the Conspiracy. He wanted to examine some of the bones stored in French museums that are more like cemeteries than cultural institutions.

"It took me two and a half years to see one bone," he told Fanny Deschamps.

"I hope it was a good one," she remarked.

"It was fascinating. At first I was told it was in a room of the Saint-Germain Museum where visitors weren't allowed. After a year and a half, when I finally got permission to look at it without touching it, it turned out not to be there anymore! *An investigation showed that it had disappeared thirty years before.* I then went through all the museums in France with a fine-toothed comb. That took me another year. At last I found the bone at the Science Faculty in Poitiers."

A year and a half to get permission to see a bone that had disappeared thirty years earlier, and no one in the museum knew it was gone! And those are the people in charge of safeguarding our prehistoric heritage, the people who pass off their mental aberrations as official doctrine and judge whether Glozel, Ica and Acambaro are genuine or not!

This little digression was necessary in order to give an understanding of the state of mind in which investigations and inquiries took place at Acambaro.

JULSRUD'S LUCKY FIND

Acambaro is a little town nestled between two mountain lakes a hundred miles northwest of Mexico City, on the road to Celayo. The site related to the culture of the Tarascos is at Chupicuaro, a short distance from the town.

It was here that in 1945 Waldemar Julsrud, a German hardware dealer, made a discovery unique in the annals of amateur archaeology: thirty-two thousand intact ceramic objects from a civilization whose existence had not even been suspected.

Julsrud was a cultivated man, curious about all sorts of things. He was keenly interested in ancient civilizations, particularly Atlantis. One day as he was riding on horseback in the foothills of the Sierra Madre, he saw on the slope of a ravine a reddish object that appeared to be a piece of pottery. He dismounted, went over to it and was delighted to discover that it was a baked clay figurine, partially buried. He easily dug it out of the ground. Odilon Tinajero, the Mexican accompanying him, dug in the surrounding area but found nothing interesting.

The figurine was strange, in an absolutely unknown style, but the two men did not pay great attention to it. They did, however, agree that Tinajero would come back to the ravine, known as El Toro, and do some more digging to determine if the figurine was isolated or part of a group.

A WHEELBARROW FULL OF FIGURINES

A few days later Tinajero came to Julsrud with a wheelbarrow loaded with statuettes of curious human beings and animals. There were thirty-eight of them, an unexpectedly large number for a preliminary probe.

Some of them represented animals that Julsrud recognized as dinosaurs, brontosaurs of the late Mesozoic era; there were also snakes, camels and lizards, and people who differed widely in their facial features, expressions, sizes, clothes and shapes.

But the most surprising part of it was that some figurines represented human beings—mostly women, recognizable by their pertly pointed breasts—who seemed to be playing with megosaurs and stegosaurs (sixty to two hundred and seventy-five million years ago), as well as crocodiles and snakes. They appeared to illustrate the Golden Age celebrated by poets, when people and animals lived together in harmony. (*See Figure 40.*)

Julsrud was overjoyed: he had the material for an important museum of his own, and he had discovered an unknown Mexican civilization.

He asked Odilon Tinajero and his two sons to begin digging at the El Toro site and promised them one peso for each complete figurine they brought him. Pieces found broken, or broken in transport, would have to be repaired by the diggers. Those that could not be repaired would not be paid for, but a record of them would have to be kept.

Considering their rate of pay, it is undeniable that the Tinajeros were exploited by Julsrud, but according to the American writer Charles H. Hapgood, he did it in order to ensure that they would excavate thoroughly and carefully. The Tinajeros were later accused of having made the figurines themselves but it is hard to imagine why they would have done so, since they would have been receiving one peso apiece for statues that each represented about a hundred pesos' worth of labor!

Thirty-two thousand intact pieces were eventually found and stored in Julsrud's house. They were everywhere: in the entrance hall, the living room, the dining room, all the bedrooms, and even the bathrooms.

This immense collection, the largest ever assembled by an archaeologist, included ceramics, stones, jades and obsidians, single subjects and scenes with several personages. The statuettes were up to three feet in height and some of the flat pieces were five feet long. The ceramics had apparently been baked over an open fire.

They were found in separate hiding places about four feet deep, each containing twenty to forty objects.

THE ENIGMATIC TARASCOS

What first intrigued Julsrud was the incredible diversity of scenes, animals and styles. Each piece had its own individuality and the collection had no unity in facial shape, clothes or decorative designs. Such designs usually make it possible to relate an object to a certain culture, but this could not be done in the case of the Acambaro figurines.

No other country in the world contains as many

different cultures as Mexico: the Toltecs, Chichimecs, Aztecs, Tlahuicas, Tarascos, Totonacs, Huastecs, Zapotecs, Mixtecs, Olmecs and Mayas, to mention only the main ones.

The Acambaro region was once the territory of the Tarascos, a mysterious people whose real name was the Tarahcues ("relatives" or "brothers-in-law"). Their language was incomprehensible to the other peoples of Mexico. It seemed to be phonetically related to the languages of Peru, where the Tarascos may have originated.

The Tarascos' buildings were also singular, composed of large platforms surmounted by *yacatas*. A *yacata* was a complex that included a circular temple joined to a pyramidal temple with a rectangular base, but this type of architecture, which can be seen mainly at Tzintzuntzan, was relatively recent. The first Tarascos remain shrouded in mystery, as do the Olmecs of the Yucatan.

The hiding places are another mystery: all the ceramics were found within an area of about an acre and a quarter. Julsrud believed they were either commercial objects stored there to await transportation, or sacred objects hidden in pits to prevent them from being taken by the Spanish conquerors. It is known that the Incas hid their wealth from Francisco Pizarro in that way.

THREE MEN WORKING A HUNDRED YEARS

Professor Charles H. Hapgood of the University of New Hampshire has honestly and conscientiously studied the Acambaro culture at the site. Other prehistorians have considered the matter and, as was to be expected, have concluded that it was a fraud perpetrated by Odilon Tinajero, though Waldemar Julsrud's honesty was not questioned. (Julsrud never profited from his collection. Once in his life he sold a few figurines to a prehistorian, but it was in order to have them shown in an exhibition.)

This is the picture presented by prehistorians: Tinajero and his two sons making thirty-two thousand ceramic objects with their own hands and baking them over a wood fire, without the knowledge of anyone in the vicinity.

It can be plausibly estimated that each of the three men would have had to work a hundred years to produce those thousands of objects and that, to bake the clay, they would have had to find tons and tons of wood, which is almost totally lacking in the Acambaro region. Furthermore the Tinajeros would have needed brilliant creative imaginations and a thorough knowledge of archaeology, zoology and paleontology. But the fact is that they barely knew how to read and write.

Yet the general opinion among "official" prehistorians was that the Acambaro collection was fraudulent. The chief reason was simple: it was unthinkable that dinosaurs from the Mesozoic era should have been living side by side with human beings, who had supposedly not come into existence until millions of years later. Other reasons, equally conclusive for the pundits, were that the objects did not belong to any known culture, that ceramics had never been known to exist for so many centuries without taking on a patina, and that such a large number of them had never been found in such a small area.

AN ATLANTEAN MUSEUM

It is true that the figurines have no clearly discernible patina, but it has been observed thousands of times that pottery preserved in a dry place (the Acambara site is quite dry) has kept its original appearance. This is the case with Roman, Greek and Egyptian pottery and the magnificent ceramics of Mochicas, Ica and

Paracas, which can be admired in the Lima Museum, and of which I own several remarkable specimens. Nearly all these ceramics still have their original color, except for the gray left by the smoke of baking, which is true of the Acambaro ceramics.

Julsrud stated that he had found remains of buried walls but his discovery does not seem to have been followed up.

The presence of dinosaurs at Acambaro does pose a problem because it is unlikely, as at Ica, that they could have found the climate and luxuriant plant life they would have needed. The region is rich in lakes, but one would have to go back hundreds of thousands of years to find an environment similar to that of the Mesozoic or the Tertiary. We must therefore assume that in Mexico, as in Peru, only a few prehistoric animals were able to survive until relatively recent times.

Or else—to return to the hypothesis suggested with regard to Ica—Acambaro was a sanctuary where Superior Ancestors had created, for the sake of future generations, a prehistoric library similar to the one discovered by Dr. Cabrera.

That was Julsrud's opinion, and he identified those who had put together the collection.

"Here," he said, "the Atlanteans left a record of their existence and made replicas of the dinosaurs that lived in the time of Atlantis."

Be that as it may, the Acambaro figurines show that an unknown civilization flourished on our planet at a time when the dinosaurs had not yet disappeared.

PROVEN AUTHENTICITY

Mexican government authorities made a long investigation at Acambaro to determine if there was any fraud. Policemen posing as archaeologists tried to pay local people to make figurines for them, and listened to conversations in taverns, but they never obtained any evidence of fraud. The conclusion of the investigation was that Julsrud's collection was genuine.

In 1972 three figurines that had been pronounced false by the American archaeologist Di Peso were tested by the thermoluminescence method in the laboratory of the University of Pennsylvania Museum. The result was conclusive: they dated from forty-five hundred years ago. Acambaro was thus authenticated, as was Glozel, and by the same method.

But stubborn pundits still deny the facts and try to discredit Julsrud's fantastic figurines.

Coming generations of enlightened prehistorians will resuscitate the ancient civilization, Atlantean or not, that, in the time of the dinosaurs, drew and sculpted the first chapters of earthly man's great adventure.

A HAZARDOUS METHOD

It has been found that various kinds of cosmic radiation are integrated into crystalline materials, notably those that enter into the composition of pottery. When a ceramic undergoes the effects of cosmic or other radiation, structural changes occur in the ring of electrons composing the clay. A laboratory procedure has been devised for studying these electrons: when they are perturbed again, they emit a quantity of light proportional to the amount received by the original radiation. Cosmic radiation is not the only kind that can affect the electrons of crystalline substances; radioactive materials on Earth produce the same phenomenon.

Dating by thermoluminescence is scarcely more precise than the carbon 14 method. I believe, however,

that work now being done on it will make it more accurate within a few years. It is already effective in
establishing that an object is quite old, but it is still
hazardous in giving an exact date. Nevertheless the age
of forty-five hundred years attributed to Julsrud's
ceramics seems satisfactory to me.

CHAPTER 6

From History to Legend

TRUTH IS A NOBLE WORD often spoken by liars, and a virtue sought by those willing to acknowledge only the theoretical and the unverifiable. May God preserve me from wanting to find Truth in the pure, romantic sense of the term!

"The truth is," a humorist once said, "that there is no truth."

And I am tempted to add, "That's true! There are only imaginings, phantasms and dreams, which the great sage Buddha called *maya* (illusion)."

It is from this viewpoint, and in this frame of mind, that I propose to examine certain points of history and legend.

ILO AND THE MOYOC MARCA

The mystery of *socabons* (tunnels and underground rooms) is not limited to South America, but in Peru it belongs to tradition in the same way as lost treasures, the Incas and secret cities.

At Ilo a rock bearing mysterious writing, now almost entirely effaced, is said to reveal the entrance to the *socabon* that leads to the lost world of the Ancients. Powerful occult defenses protect that mysterious world, where gold and precious stones abound.

Such legends circulate all over the country, and the Peruvians are particularly fond of them. It is said that a vast underground passage goes from Lima to Cuzco and that the ancient capital of the Incas is connected to the fortress of Sacsahuaman, which overlooks the city, by *socabons* forming a labyrinth in which the treasure of the Incas is hidden. I can readily believe in that secret sanctuary where Huascar, the last of the lawful Inca rulers, buried the wealth of his kingdom when the greedy Spaniards invaded the empire and crossed—the devil only knows how—the "uncrossable" Andes.

The entrance to the labyrinth was in the Moyoc Marca, a kind of stronghold that rose from the center of the fortress. A priestly caste composed of members of the Council of Elders had charge of the underground city. The network of passages was so ingeniously designed that not even the king—the Inca—could go into the city without being guided.

The heart of the labyrinth was an immense cavern where an abundant spring had its origin.

THE ENCLOSURE OF GOLD

The treasures of the kingdom are said to have been hidden at the center of the labyrinth, which the conquistadores were never able to reach because its guardians had blocked the secret passages by making them collapse.

This is the hiding place of the world's most fantastic treasure, the "Enclosure of Gold," of which Garcilaso de La Vega has given us a fascinating description.

> But above all these wonders appeared fields of maize made with perfect realism, with their roots, blossoms and ears, whose points were of gold and the rest of silver, all brazed together.... There were also large and small animals made of gold and silver, such as rabbits, rats, lizards, snakes, butterflies, foxes, wildcats (they had no domestic cats), birds of all sorts, some seeming to sing as they perched on trees and others spreading their wings as though to fly, deer, lions, tigers; in short, all kinds of animals each made to look perfectly natural and placed in its normal setting.
>
> All the houses had bathrooms with large gold and silver tubs in which the Incas washed themselves, and the pipes that brought in water were of the same metals. They had also placed beautiful gold decorations at places where there were springs with naturally hot water, which they used for their baths. ...
>
> As soon as they saw the Spaniards' insatiable lust for gold and silver, the Indians hid most of their treasure so well that none of it has ever been found, and it is unlikely that any of it ever will be found, except perhaps by accident, for it is certain that the Indians of today do not know where that treasure is, and that their ancestors left them no clue to its location, to make sure that those things would never be used by anyone but their kings, for whom they were exclusively intended.

The treasure, whose value is no doubt exaggerated, is said to be hidden in the secret city of Sacsahuaman, near the spring known only to the Inca and the members of the Council of Elders.

THE CAVE: WOMB AND LIBRARY

As long as there have been human beings, there has been the myth of the cave, the underground passages leading to it, and the material or spiritual treasures hidden in it.

The symbolism of the myth is obvious: the entrance to the cave is woman's vagina; the passages are the tubes that lead to it; the treasure is either physical potency or the subtle alchemy that results in creation of the fetus.

Moreover it is known that the human cycle begins at the wondrous cave of Eve-Lilith, passes to the more spacious cave of the Mater's belly, then back to the wondrous cave, and finally to the stone cave of the Earth Mother, where people have always buried their dead in the fetal position.

It is thus easy to understand the importance of the cave in esotericism, why prehistoric people were reluctant to part with their stone caves, and why they hid their most precious possessions in them: statuettes, vases, flint tools and specimens of their writing.

All the first documents of human history are in caves or underground rooms. This is man's tribute to the womb of the Earth Mother, a womb whose spell he cannot break: it permeates, animates and inspires him from birth to death. (The Christian religion considers this magic and occultism pernicious and has struggled against it.)

The child in danger takes refuge against his mother's belly and pulls her apron over his head to give himself the illusion of the darkness and security of the womb.

The sage (or pseudosage) who wants to "fulfill" himself, and return into himself, goes to meditate in the cave of initiation, which the Egyptians represented as a snake forming an enclosure.

It was in the caves of Qumran that the Essenes hid their writings, now known as the Dead Sea Scrolls. It

In the Egyptian rite the neophyte was depicted as enclosed in a snake forming a cave of initiation.

was in caves in Europe, South America, North America, Africa and Australia that ancient peoples left records of their existence. And it was in caves that mysteries and initiations took place, conspirators and fugitives gathered, and priestesses made their predictions.

"Human beings are fully realized in the primordial cave," writes Jean-Pierre Bayard.

THE ARCHIVES OF THE WORLD ARE IN SECRET SANCTUARIES

It was thus in underground sanctuaries that the people of ancient Ica stored their records of the knowledge that had been transmitted to them by mysterious Instructors. But the Primohistoric Library of Ica is not unique in the world, and perhaps not even in the Andes.

In the nineteenth century Elena Petrovna Blavatsky, a visionary woman who was truly an Initiate, wrote a revealing book that became the bible of theosophists: *The Secret Doctrine*. Its teachings, comprising the annals of a people unknown to archaeologists, are said to be older than the Vedas. In it she states (and I can readily believe her) that long ago there was a primordial revelation that was hidden in different parts of the world. It was written in the mother language that was the direct ancestor of Sanskrit. It will reappear some day, which leads us to assume that it has always been piously kept by chains of Initiates, or at least that they kept it a very long time, perhaps adding accounts of more recent events to the original text.

This would explain why Dr. Cabrera's stones are able to recount the great human adventure from the Mesozoic to the Christian era, of which it gives us certain disturbing echoes. Since thousands of the stones still remain to be discovered, some of them, if this view is correct, ought to represent fairly recent scenes, people and events.

More conversant with Oriental civilization than with that of the Amerindian countries, Blavatsky writes that after the destruction of the Alexandrian Library, many of whose parchments were fortunately saved, copies were made by initiated scholars, and these sacred books of human history are in highly secret esoteric schools in India, Tibet, China, the Near East *and South America*.

THE ENTRANCES ARE HIDDEN AND CANNOT BE DISCOVERED

Blavatsky situates several of these secret sanctuaries in underground crypts and library caves carved out of solid rock beneath great lamaseries and hermitages built in high mountains, in the passes of the Kunlun Mountains in northern Tibet, along the Tarim River in western China and near Okkee Math in the Himalayas.

She says that in the underground rooms of a temple in the gorge of the Altyntagh, pilgrims have seen ancient books so numerous that the British Museum could not contain them. This is an exaggerated statement, but it is probably based on a real report, as is the story of a buried city, known only to Mongols and Buddhists, whose vast underground residences contain clay tablets and cylinders.

According to Blavatsky, the Bible of Moses is only a compilation of much older writings, notably those of the Chaldean Magi, of which nothing remains but the fragments quoted by Berossus. She also mentions a "very old book" written on cloth of an unknown nature, from which were copied the *Siphrah Dzeniutha,* the *Sepher Jezirah,* the *Pentateuch* of the Hebrews, the Chaldean *Book of Numbers,* the Chinese *Shu-Ching* and the Hindu *Puranas.* This mysterious book was written in Senzar, the sacred language of the Toltecs, the Atlanteans and Initiates all over the world.

The Chaldean annals are said to cover a period of two hundred thousand years but, as in the case of Sanchuniathon's *Phoenician History* and Manetho's *Synchronistic Tables,* the manuscripts have either been lost or interpolated by Christian writers, particularly Eusebius, Bishop of Caesarea, who was denounced as "the most impudent of falsifiers" by Socrates (the fifth-century church historian, not the Greek philosopher).

Blavatsky says that the storage rooms are deep underground, and that their entrances are so well hidden that they cannot be discovered.

BLAVATSKY AND DR. CABRERA

In the nineteenth century, according to Blavatsky, there were documents in the Imperial Library of Saint

Petersburg (now Leningrad) stating that Russian mystics crossed the Ural Mountains and went to Tibet to seek initiation and knowledge in unknown crypts in central Asia.

She thus refers to the hidden sanctuaries that people have been seeking all over the world for the past two thousand years, in the hope of finding the archives of vanished races, and also jewels and gold statuettes and vases more fabulous than those of the Indian maharajahs.

Since the time of Sanchuniathon the Phoenician, who discovered Ammonian writings relating the ancient history of Egypt and the Near East, no one has given proof of a genuine discovery of this kind, except for Dr. Cabrera, whose stones seem to belong to one of those secret sanctuaries that were kept and enriched by a long series of esotericists.

Blavatsky never showed the documents on which she based *The Secret Doctrine,* but the unquestionable value of her revelations favors the assumption that she was sincere. It is up to inspired esotericists to determine if there is any real correspondence between the underground sanctuaries described in *The Secret Doctrine* and the caves of Ocucaje, where Dr. Cabrera's stones were found.

VON DÄNIKEN CAME CLOSE

My friend Erich von Däniken has extraordinary premonitions! Although he did not discover it, he sensed the existence of the Primohistoric Library of Ica, and he says that he went into an underground cavity where the Superior Ancestors hid a museum for the benefit of future peoples.

This story was published by the excellent Peruvian journalist Zizi Ghenea—with great reservations, it must be admitted.

"To tell you the truth, I don't believe it," she said

to me. "Von Däniken always finds amazing things that are never seen by anyone else and can't be verified."

Be that as it may, here is what Zizi Ghenea wrote about the underground kingdom in Peru, which is supposedly a counterpart of the Agartha* in Tibet, and perhaps of the secret city that is said to lie at the bottom of a Venezuelan crater and in the adjacent caves.

Joan Moricz, an Argentinian adventurer of Hungarian origin, says that in 1970 he discovered a fantastic network of underground passages connecting Ecuador and Peru at a depth of about six hundred feet. When von Däniken learned of this in March 1971, he took a plane to Peru, determined to exploit Moricz's discovery. Moricz welcomed him enthusiastically. He was glad to have his story believed—but on condition that he did not have to prove it by telling where the passages were!

He tried to dissuade von Däniken from carrying out his plan. When his efforts failed, he agreed to give him the location of an unimportant secondary entrance that was known to many of the local people and a large number of Ecuadorian archaeologists. It was near Cuenca, about sixty miles southeast of Guayaquil.

Did von Däniken find the real underground passages through that entrance? It is impossible to have any certainty on the subject because neither von Däniken nor Moricz nor his assistant Gerardo Peña Mathaus has produced the slightest proof of their discoveries.

A TRUTH EMBEDDED IN FICTION

Nevertheless there were rumors, which Zizi Ghenea reported in the magazine *Dominical*: "Joan Moricz

---

* In Indian tradition, the Agartha is a vast underground city under the Himalayas. Its existence was revealed to Ossendowski by a monk named Turgut. Its location is approximately 88° east longitude and 28° north latitude, near Shigatse, Tibet. (See my books *One Hundred Thousand Years of Man's Unknown History* and *Masters of the World*.)

had said that the Peruvian-Ecuadorian passage contained objects of great value and records showing the existence of an ancient advanced civilization that disappeared before or during the Deluge. Von Däniken was sure there was a hiding place containing such things, but he had to find out where it was."

Von Däniken wrote in one of his books that he had actually found the tunnel and that in it he had seen gold statues of unknown animals and manuscripts written on sheets of gold.

"But," said the magazine *Nostradamus,* "Joan Moricz denied the truth of this statement and said that Von Däniken had never been in the tunnel containing priceless documents."

The German magazine *Stern* also contacted Moricz and was told that Von Däniken's story was false.

A scientific expedition guided by the geologist Otto G. Geyer concluded, after an investigation, that the report was simply imaginary.

If Von Däniken and Moricz invented their stories out of whole cloth, they must be credited with the brilliant feat of imagining a truth that it was impossible for them to discover! For the tunnel exists, even though it is only a cave and a group of underground passages, even though its entrance is not at Cuenca, but in Peru: it exists at Ocucaje, twenty miles south of Ica.

STONES THAT NO ONE WILL EVER SEE

Yes, there really is a sanctuary where the Superior Ancestors of an unknown, vanished civilization stored their archives, a summary of their knowledge and the true history of mankind. It was found by Dr. Cabrera. And I am proud that I, in turn, discovered Dr. Cabrera and the new place where the stones are kept.

Others invent; I tell the truth, with supporting evidence: the museum is at Bolivar 170, Plaza de Armas, in Ica; the sanctuary is near Ocucaje; I have published several photographs of message-stones from the antediluvian world, pending publication of Dr. Cabrera's book, which will become the new bible of mankind and will reveal nearly all the mysteries of our Superior Ancestors.

I have revealed secrets and given proof of the discovery; for example, by showing the essential phases of a heart transplant without the phenomenon of rejection.

But I have not told everything.

The revelations of the Ica stones are infinitely more disturbing and incredible than I am at liberty to say. It is for Dr. Cabrera alone to publish most of the engravings, but I can now say that, *for extremely valid reasons, he will not divulge all the messages.* Those stones are a legacy from great Initiates to a great Initiate, and so there is necessarily an area that must not be revealed, except to a very small number of adepts.

Dr. Cabrera has shown certain "dangerous" engravings to Robert Laffont and Francis Mazière, but I can state that neither of those two men has seen the most important stones, that they do not even know of their existence and that probably no one but Dr. Cabrera and I will ever see them.

THE EARTH MOTHER
OPENS HER WOMBS

In our time of apocalypse (revelation) strange scenes take place in the air, people are struggling to know the truth and the bowels of the earth are opening to divulge secrets that have been hidden for thousands of years.

For several decades Gaea, the Earth Mother, has been giving birth to mummified fetuses of humanoids and people of ancient times, bringing forth cities whose existence was previously unsuspected, giving glimpses, in her womb scars, of fantastic visions she may have spawned in her delirium.

Emile Fradin brings Glozel to light, Waldemar Julsrud finds thirty-two thousand ceramics in Mexico, Javier Cabrera Darquea discovers the Ica stones. And, at a lower level, Von Däniken and Moricz sense the existence of the real underground Agartha.

A few years ago a French Initiate, Raymond Bernard, Grand Master of AMORC, clearly revealed that the Agartha is no longer in Tibet. He probably made a more detailed statement to trustworthy adepts.

THE AGARTHA OF VENEZUELA

The Agartha, that mysterious underground kingdom that, according to the writer Ossendowski, lies under the Himalayas, is now in South America if we are to believe certain traditions. It was perhaps this South American Agartha that Harry Gibson, a Venezuelan pilot, saw during a routine flight in 1964, at the bottom of two craters in the jungle somewhere between the Sierra Maigualida and the Orinoco River.

It is a strange story, and one would be tempted to place it in the same category as reports of imaginary kingdoms—El Dorado, Paititi, Moricz's tunnel—if it had not been taken very seriously by two respected archaeologists, David Nott of Liverpool and Charles Brewer Carias of Caracas, assisted by the Venezuelan Air Force and ten scientists from different nations.

The craters are near the sources of the rivers Caura and Ventuari, and two mountains known as Pava and Masiati, at the edge of the Sierra Pacaraima. The volcanoes have been extinct for thousands or perhaps millions of years, so scientists hope to find plant and animal life in them that has long since disappeared from the rest of the world.

In January 1974 a first three-member team went down into one of the craters, about a thousand feet deep and twelve hundred feet wide. They brought back living plants and animals of species that were either unknown or had been thought extinct since the Mesozoic.

The two craters are connected by an underground passage nearly a mile long. According to unverified rumors, it is still in use, because traces of recent activity were found in it.

So much for the openly announced part of the discovery. The most important results are being kept secret by the Venezuelan scientific authorities, for mysterious reasons. This secrecy has given rise to private inquiries among the people living in the surrounding mountains, whose local names are Jaua-Jidi and Sari Inama-Jidi. Fantastic legends concerning the mystery of the two craters have been gathered.

THE LOST PARADISE AT
THE BOTTOM OF A VOLCANO

The region of Jaua-Jidi is a dense, very sparsely inhabited forest. It has been difficult for Venezuelan investigators to make contact with the primitive people who live there. They shun outsiders, speak an unknown language and do not understand Spanish. Halfbreeds from the town of Esmeralda, on the Orinoco, have been able to approach them, however.

"Strange people wearing strange clothes have been seen several times in the forest of Jaua-Jidi," one of them reported. "They seem unwilling to approach the Indians and they venture only a short distance away from the craters. Their skin is the color of yellowed ivory; they have big eyes, like a jaguar's, and long hair of different colors. They seem fearful and run away whenever they hear an unusual sound. They are thought to live at the bottoms of the craters and in vast underground rooms, with secret entrances in the forest."

Other reports would seem to indicate that the people of the "Kingdom of Two Craters" are in almost constant contact with space beings, but it should be pointed out that sightings of flying saucers are more common in Central and South America than anywhere else in the world.

The Indians of the forest say that at night the trees on the rim of each volcano are illuminated by a soft green light that apparently comes from the bottom. Occasionally something that looks like a "little round airplane" comes out of the darkness, enters the green halo and disappears into the volcano.

Two or three nights before David Nott, Brewer Carias, G. Dunsterville and their companions came to the site, intense activity by the flying "things" was observed. They were as numerous as a swarm of bees but, perhaps because of their distance from the observers, they flew without making any discernible sound.

The Indians felt that the strange people were receiving heavy reinforcements, or else that they were moving out before the archaeologists came. In any case they left little trace of their presence in the underground passages, but enough to give convincing evidence that their existence is not a myth. The Indians believe that the "Kingdom of Two Craters" extends under the mountains and that, for the time being, its entrances are tightly closed.

In Lima Zizi Ghenea told me that a little forest of trees extinct everywhere else grew inside the caves and the craters, and that in it lived animals from the Tertiary.

What is strange about this whole affair, in which legend is mingled with fact, is the Venezuelan government's inexplicable silence and the secrecy in which the expedition's report has been kept.

NARCISSO GENOVESE'S
SCIENTIFIC CENTER

Is there a correlation between the Kingdom of Two Craters and the Underground City of the Andes or, as it is called in Spanish, the Ciudad Subterranea de los Andes (CSA), which is discussed in private from Caracas to Santiago?

Here again, as in the case of von Däniken's crypts and the underground people of Jaua-Jidi, we can refer only to unverifiable rumors and stories told by pseudo-initiates with a penchant for extraterrestrial mysteries. Yet a Mexican journalist named Mario Rojas Avendaro investigated the story of the CSA, added his own embellishments and inventions, and finally, like Von Däniken, revealed genuine secrets when he thought he was imagining the plot of a science-fiction novel!

He wrote his story on the basis of statements supposedly made to him by a former disciple of Guglielmo Marconi: Narcisso Genovese, a physicist, philologist and teacher at a high school in Baja California, Mexico.

According to Genovese, when Marconi died in 1937 his students decided to continue his work on the utilization of solar or cosmic energy, taking all possible precautions to make sure it would not be used for war or criminal purposes. Ninety-eight scientists and technicians from various countries formed an organization similar to the Pugwash Committee and withdrew to a deserted region of the Andes (or of the forest), where they lived isolated and unknown.

Their work consists in taming the electrical forces of space in the service of a peaceful, universal goal. The community is governed by three basic principles:

—One religion on Earth: that of the true God, or Universal Intelligence.

—One nation: the planet Earth.

—One policy: worldwide peace and an alliance with the peoples of space.

Possessing large financial resources (taken, it is said, from the war treasuries of Benito Mussolini and Adolf Hitler), the association has built an underground city with better research facilities than any other installation in the world.

HELP FROM MARS

According to Genovese's report, the scientific advance of the CSA comes from aid given by space people who have a base on Mars. These extraterrestrials visit the Andes scientists and have helped them to build several spacecraft.

In 1946 the center was already using a powerful collector of cosmic energy, the essential component of all matter, in Marconi's theories.

Genovese states that at the first stage of research, the physicists of the CSA counted on the antagonism between matter and antimatter. They now draw energy directly from the sun.

"In 1952," he says, "we traveled above all the seas and continents in a craft whose energy supply was continuous and practically inexhaustible. It reached a speed of half a million miles an hour and withstood enormous pressures, near the limit of resistance of the alloys that composed it. The problem was to slow it down at just the right time.

"We had our first contact with extraterrestrials from Mars on December 16, 1955, at five o'clock in the afternoon. We had already sent radio and light signals. We were surprised to see a formation of five craft flying over our camp."

(The CSA is sometimes a secret city and sometimes a "camp." The whole story is extremely dubious. The technical and scientific details are vague and would seem to indicate that the CSA is behind European and American technology, rather than ahead of it. I am publishing the story without attaching any value to it, other than as a messianic and premonitory phenomenon, and as an expression of desire-images.)

"When we sent radio signals to them, one of the craft prepared to land while the others hovered above us, keeping watch and ready to serve as a cover if necessary. The craft we contacted was a flying saucer. It radiated phosphorescent light that disappeared when its propulsion system was turned off. On the ground it took on a fantastic, opaque, light brown color."

Genovese continues his account by describing the saucer. It had a diameter of about twenty-five feet and was surrounded by a smooth rim that rotated when the craft was in motion.

As in many stories of this kind, the extraterrestrial visitors were tall, pale and blue-eyed and wore tight one-piece costumes made of an unknown material. And, of course, they had higher, broader and more rounded foreheads than earthlings.

GENOVESE IS IGNORANT OF GEOGRAPHY

Conversation took place by means of a computer that "reflected the electric waves of the earthlings' brains, thus transmitting their thoughts, which were naturally decoded by the better-organized brains of the extraterrestrials."

A celestial map and globe were used to show the location of the planet from which the visitors had come: Mars, known as Loga in their language.

This part of the story clearly shows that it was fabricated: Mars is said to have a larger population than Earth, one that is technologically far superior to us. But after the photographs sent back by Mariner 9, we can consider it certain that Mars is uninhabited, at least on its surface, since its sandy soil, swept by horrendous winds, does not lend itself to any kind of construction.

The pseudo-Genovese nevertheless assures us that Martians and earthlings now exchange scientific information and visits in flying saucers propelled by solar energy. On Mars there is only one nation, one social class and one universe-god, whose name is Sundi.

All this would be wonderfully encouraging if Genovese, a "learned physicist, philologist and humanist," did not show himself to be an inept geographer by adding: "A month later the Center for Space Studies, located in the tropical forest of the Andes at an altitude of thirteen thousand feet, was visited a second time."

I have traveled in the Andes from the Chilean border to the region of San Agustin and from Bogotá to Colombia, and I have flown over their entire length many times. I can state from personal observation that there are no tropical forests at an altitude of thirteen thousand feet, but only bare rocks and stunted vegetation.

My conclusion is that the stories of Genovese and Mario Rojas are false, *even if they are not totally groundless.*

THE DREAMED TRUTH
OF LIARS AND MESSIAHS

That statement might seem odd and contradictory if several elements did not give it a certain consistency.

First of all, I am not far from believing that there are special reasons why the Andes, and particularly Peru, should be chosen by possible if not *probable* extraterrestrial visitors.

A Mexican journalist clumsily launches myths of a secret city in the Andes, brotherly harmony between the peoples of Earth and Mars, an interplanetary nation, the replacement of the old, bearded God of the West by a universe-god. All this belongs to the latent dream of twentieth-century people and the desire-images that they condense. Mediums like Von Däniken take in those images and feel themselves called upon to play the part of messiahs.

Study of the phenomenon shows that messiahs, false or genuine, belong to true history, even if it is occult or has not yet happened. In short, I believe that the "inventions" of writers in search of startling stories correspond to a premonitory truth, that this was the case with the prehistoric library imagined by Von Däniken, and that it may be the case with the Underground City of the Andes, which logically succeeds the ancient and outdated Agartha.

And it is strange that the Mexican journalist, obviously not very familiar with science, logic or geography, should have had enough knowledge to invent the physicist Genovese, a disciple of Guglielmo Marconi. For there is a very real mystery concerning Marconi.

MARCONI'S FANTASTIC INVENTION

In 1937 the great Italian scientist's death from a heart attack seemed mysterious to many of his compatriots.

Marconi was certainly one of the greatest geniuses of his time, since, with the aid of Hertz's spark arrester, Popov's antenna and Branly's coherer, he made the first radio transmission in 1895. What is less well known about his work is his discovery of what would now be called a death ray, as reported by Rachele Mussolini, widow of the Italian dictator Benito Mussolini.

One afternoon in June 1936 she was traveling by car to Ostia, where she had a small estate. That morning her husband, who knew about her trip, had told her to be on the road from Rome to Ostia between three o'clock and three-thirty. "You'll see something that will surprise you," he had said with a mysterious expression.

Intrigued, she did as he said, and at exactly three o'clock her car stopped for no apparent reason. At first she thought it was an ordinary mechanical breakdown, especially since her chauffeur lifted the hood of the car and began tinkering with the engine. But then she saw that all the other cars on the road had also stopped. Dozens of drivers were calling out to each other, unscrewing parts of their cars, blowing into tubes, activating fuel pumps. As far as the eye could see, not a single car was moving. It was bewildering and a little frightening.

"I don't understand what's happened," said Rachele's chauffeur. "It's as if someone cast a spell on this road!"

After what her husband had told her, she felt confident. She shrugged her shoulders and said that if the car did not start within half an hour they would have a wrecker come and tow it away. Around her, drivers were swearing and looking puzzled.

At three-thirty-five she told her chauffeur to try the engine again. To his amazement, it started and ran perfectly. The other cars also began moving. After half an hour of suspense, everything resumed as if nothing had happened.

That evening Mussolini gave his wife the key to the mystery by telling her that an ultrasecret experiment had been performed with an invention by Marconi, who had devised a system of rays that could disrupt the electrical circuits of engines. Mussolini believed that this would give Italy decisive superiority in case of war. He even believed that, with further research, Marconi's invention could be made effective against living beings and would thus become a death ray.

HE RECEIVED MESSAGES FROM SPACE

In March 1930, assisted by the physicist Landini, Marconi performed experiments aboard his yacht *Elec-*

tra, which had been made into a floating laboratory. He is said to have succeeded in sending wave trains from Genoa to Australia, where electric lights went on for no discernible reason.

It is said that Pope Pius XI learned about the invention of paralyzing rays in 1936 and that, regarding it as satanic, he took steps to have Mussolini order Marconi to stop such research and destroy all records of it. A year later Marconi died in a way that many of those who knew him considered unclear, but it may be assumed that his close collaborators knew about his work and had a copy of his records. It can probably be stated that Marconi was keenly interested in the question of extraterrestrial civilizations and had received signals, if not messages, from space people.

It is interesting to note that the Mexican journalist who wrote the article on the Underground City of the Andes, and who seems to be totally ignorant in scientific matters, was shrewd enough to include a disciple of Marconi in a story that otherwise does not appear to deserve the slightest credence. Such stories or legends have been persistently circulating in South America for many years and may, in some respects, be related to the mystery of the "Kingdom of Two Craters."

Narcisso Genovese claims that extraterrestrials have been interested in earthly affairs since 1917 and that several of them are living among us. They have great difficulty adjusting to our atmosphere, which explains why they choose to stay in the Andes, where the air is less dense than at lower altitudes.

Genovese gives a detailed description of a trip he made to Mars, and he names the scientists of the CSA and the research center on Mars, but it goes without saying that none of his assertions can be verified. It is beyond question, however, that his descriptions of life on Mars are completely incompatible with the photographs sent back by American space probes. The pseudoscientific drawings and explanations in Mario Rojas's articles are also inadmissible to space scientists.

We should be highly skeptical of these stories, to say the least, but we should not lose sight of the possibility that they may involve a premonitory phenomenon.

PIERRE VOGEL FINDS A SUBMERGED CITY

Pierre Vogel, a diver who lives in Marseilles, believes in vanished civilizations and his faith is strengthened by a sensational discovery that he recently made in the Mediterranean.

Fascinated by underwater adventure, Vogel (see Figure 41) has a diving equipment store on the Marseilles waterfront and spends all his spare time on the sea bottom. No one knows the shoals of the Marseilles region as well as he does.

One day when he was cruising in the five miles of sea between two islands, the Ile Maire and the Ile du Planier, he passed over the Veyron, a shoal forty feet below the surface, well known to underwater fisherman and dreaded by sailors. The sea can be rough in that area, and captains of large ships are advised not to come within a mile and a half of the Veyron. There are interconnected caves all over the shoal.

Vogel had dived there perhaps a hundred times before, as though in answer to some sort of mysterious call. On this day he finally understood. And the illumination that struck him was the result of a whole series of observations and careful studies. There could be no doubt of it: the Veyron was a submerged city!

"The first time I dived there, I was struck by the layout of the tunnels in the shoal," he told me.

There were several features that could be explained only as products of human work, particularly the network of tunnels that intersect at right angles, with a large central "crossroads." Their ceilings are perfectly straight, and in some places there are adjoining semispherical rooms with cylindrical chimneys that go through ten to twenty feet of rock. The whole site covers about a hundred thousand square feet.

After taking mineral samples, Vogel became convinced that the Veyron was a prehistoric city where iron had been smelted. The semispherical rooms were furnaces controlled by means of tunnels, at the ends of which deposits of slag were found. The walls of the tunnels were examined by mineralogists and found to have a high iron content that could be explained only by the flow of molten metal.

Smelting was done in the western part of the city. In the eastern part there are no furnaces or chimneys, only tunnels where anchors were carved from a kind of black stone that is not found in the surrounding area.

PERHAPS HOMER'S BASILEA

"The coastal region," Pierre Vogel told me, "is rich in underwater caves, more than sixty feet below the surface, which have been officially recognized by prehistorians. That's true of the Tremies cave at Port-Miou, for example. It was inhabited less than thirty thousand years ago. Then it was submerged when the level of the sea rose suddenly.

"Briefly, this is how I see my discovery: Thirty thousand years ago, people lived on an island about four miles from the nearest coast and half a mile from a rocky mass that later became the Planier reef. Those prehistoric people smelted iron and worked with stone that came from two hundred miles away, near Collioure.

"Although I have no proof, I called my discovery the 'Basilea civilization,' by analogy with the Basilea in Homer's stories."

(In the *Odyssey* Homer speaks of a Greco-Pelasgian city on an island near the mainland, where Vulcan's blacksmiths, the one-eyed Cyclopses, forged metal in caves.)

Professor Valentine, an expert on the submerged ruins at Bimini, in the Bahamas, is interested in "Basilea" and feels certain that ancient worlds were swallowed up by the sea on several different occasions, which is an opinion rejected by a number of official prehistorians but shared by nearly all traditionalists and "maverick" archaeologists.

Henri de Lumley, a professor at the University of Marseilles, has stated that three hundred thousand years ago the Mediterranean was eighty-five feet higher than it is today, and four degrees cooler. It later underwent earthquakes and geological convulsions that sometimes lowered its level and sometimes raised it.

From material found at Port-Miou, it is certain that land that is now about a hundred feet below the surface of the Mediterranean was above it thirty thousand years ago. Logically, Pierre Vogel's "Basilea" should be placed in that same period. That would add some twenty-seven thousand years to the duration of the Iron Age, which textbooks are not ashamed to state began in 1500 B.C.!

If the submerged city of the Veyron is officially recognized, France will share with the Andes region and Soviet Armenia (Medzamor) the privilege of having witnessed the first Iron Age.

Meanwhile, of course, other discoveries prove the existence of our Superior Ancestors and give evidence of errors in the conventional version of prehistory.

THE CARVED ROCKS OF LA VAULX

The La Vaulx site, in the Deux-Sèvres department of France, is not a recent discovery, but it shows the negligence of our pundits. Who has ever heard of the carved rocks of La Vaulx? Who has ever seen the six fine specimens that disappeared into the Museum of Saint-Germain-en-Laye at the beginning of this century? Yet, from an archaeological viewpoint, La Vaulx is as important as Carnac, Filitosa and Mount Bego, and it surpasses them in artistic value.

The site was discovered about 1850 by the Marquis de la Bretesche, who reported it, in vain, to Monsieur Parenteau, curator of the Nantes Archaeological Museum. Its importance was first recognized by Abbé Théophile Gabard of Saint-Aubin-de-Baubigné, soon after the turn of the century. He made copies of the carvings and, in 1908, wrote what he knew on the subject.

La Vaulx is about a mile and a half from the little town of Saint-Aubin-de-Baubigné. In this green, hilly countryside the gray, rounded backs of Jurassic granite rocks rise from the ground in meadows and moors. It was probably their smoothness that prompted people in remote times to carve the essentials of their knowledge on them: the stars, woman as lover and mother, the symbols of their pagan religion.

The carvings belong to the same type of culture as those of Cachão do Algarve in Portugal, Vallecamonica in Italy and Mount Bego in the Alpes-Maritimes department of France, but they are more elaborate, which does not prove that they are more recent.

According to old reports, many stones bearing particularly complex and skillfully executed carvings disappeared in the nineteenth century. About fifty stones and two hundred carvings still remain.

Louis Capitan, the prehistorian who tried to discredit the Glozel site, estimated the age of the La Vaulx culture at about twenty-five hundred years. I personally believe it is at least five thousand years old, and more likely six or seven thousand.

THE LADY OF LA VAULX

Each carving has a rare artistic quality and a sureness of line that belong only to the engravers of prehistoric times.

One of the finest, even though it is only a stylized, anonymous figure, is the strikingly elegant and suggestive "Lady of La Vaulx." As if to add to her radiance, lichen has given her a smiling mouth, a white, clinging dress and a brightly colored flower that seems to serve as a fastener for her dress. (*See Figure 42.*)

"She looks like a cabaret singer offering her body to two giant hands," remarked my friend Jean Pastré, an archaeologist.

The contours of the rocks are often incorporated into the design of the carvings, a technique that was common in prehistoric times.

There are several signs or symbols: stars, lines, almond-shaped figures that may represent either eyes or vulvae, large and small circles, angles, spirals, crosses, rectangles, as well as human and animal figures.

A rock in the shape of an altar, bearing a circle divided by a horizontal and a vertical line, suggests sun worship. (*See Figure 43.*)

The stars may be an indication of star worship but they may also commemorate the arrival of the comet-planet Venus, which would date the carvings at five thousand years ago.

It is possible that the large circles symbolize the sun, and the almond-shaped figures the moon or the vulva, but it should be noted that no phallic signs appear at La Vaulx.

The lines, nearly all horizontal, suggest several possible explanations: numbers, days, years, stairs, deaths, etc.

In symbolism, a vertical line often indicates a living man and a horizontal one a dead or reclining man.

One carved rock is under the floor of a farmhouse,

another is incorporated into a stone wall, and a third is at the edge of a road in front of a farm building. The Lady of La Vaulx is in a meadow.

Like the civilization of Mount Bego, Bimini, Acambaro and Ica, that of La Vaulx may have emerged from its nebulous past to witness and announce the end of an age.

CHAPTER 7

Samirza the Extraterrestrial
and the Sierra of Silence

WHILE MARIO ROJAS had a premonition of events that will supposedly take place in about the year 2000, Joan Moricz and Erich von Däniken only absorbed ancient traditions well known to esotericists.

BIBLES ON GOLD TABLETS

Those who are willing to believe something simply on the basis of a statement, especially if the statement is in print, maintain that the mysterious gold tablets of the Gobi Desert* are the archives of the ancient world.

---

* Oriental traditions also mention "pearls" of the Gobi Desert, which have been identified as initiatory revelations. But, perhaps in correlation with these traditions, it is interesting to note that in 1973 a Soviet archaeological expedition discovered in the Gobi Desert (which was once a sea) fossil pearls a hundred million years old according to geochronology. They were still "alive," and it is known that pearls "die" after three to four hundred million years.

Who found those tablets? Even though the legend dates only from the nineteenth century, its origin is already veiled by obscurity and confusion.

Who has seen them? No one!

Written in an unknown language, they are said to tell the story of the Land of Mu before the worldwide Deluge and the arrival of the Masters of the World, who came from the sky. Their most secret revelations will not be made public till the End of Time!

The tablets have disappeared. Were they stolen? Did they fly away? Were they taken up into the sky? One version says that the gold tablets were taken to several sanctuaries, where they were transmuted into copper.

The history of the ancient world that Sanchuniathon read on gold tablets (or in a book, it has also been said) shows how important it is for everything valuable to be made durable. This is probably the origin of the idea of writing on a metal that does not rust or corrode. It is probably also the origin of the myth (not necessarily groundless) of all those apocalyptic accounts bequeathed to posterity in the same way. But it has been proven that in transmitting a highly important message the worst mistake is to write it on a precious metal which, though it resists rust and corrosion, is worth a great deal of money and is therefore almost certain to be stolen and melted down.

Von Däniken was not convinced of that, since he looked for thousands of thin gold tablets in Joan Moricz's phantom *socabon*. But perhaps he had heard of the Gobi messages or the saga of the winged god Samirza Yao-Ha, also called Samirza Rucatl, Mirtcha, or the Great Ancestor.

THE *BOOK OF*
THE CHILDREN OF THE SUN

My friend Jimmy Guieu, a renowned science-fiction writer and a great specialist on the subject of UFOs and extraterrestrials, has revealed that saga in his excellent book *Le Livre du Paranormal*.

Guieu is undoubtedly one of the best-informed esotericists of our time, and it is possible that in the future his books, *especially his science-fiction stories,* will come to be regarded as the most accurate prophetic works of the twentieth century. I consider him a genuinely inspired writer, a medium, and it is certain that mystery goes to him as water flows to the sea. One proof of this is the saga of the winged god, which I would not have known if he had not brought it to my attention.

This saga, which recounts the primohistory of the human race, was originally written on thin gold tablets. Its present preserver, Lysianne Delsol, of Montaren, France, has given me a summary of it.

"I do not know," she writes, "who brought that tradition into our family, but it was faithfully transmitted and has belonged to us since time immemorial.

"I have been told that at first it was a story written on gold tablets in an unknown language that appeared to be numerical, and that an accurate translation of it existed. The very thin tablets, bound together by rings, formed a kind of book called *Thor Heliohim,* or *Book of the Children of the Sun.* It was confiscated by the Inquisition.

"Although that book really existed, no one in my family has ever known what became of it, whether it was melted down, stolen, destroyed or hidden. The story was a kind of poem emanating from the demigod Jika, or Jimkhy or Simchy."

THE ANGELS WERE SKILLFUL LOVERS

According to Jimmy Guieu, the saga of the ancient solar tradition is an expansion, prudently effaced by the Church, of the sixth verse of *Genesis.*

Samirza Rucatl Heliohim, the "god who came from the stars," strangely recalls Samyaza who, in the third chapter of the *Book of Enoch,* is the leader of the angels who came down to Earth to make love with earthly women. (See Chapter 6 of my book *Legacy of the Gods.*)

Like his angelic counterpart, Samirza brought earthlings the superior knowledge of peoples of the sky, not only in industrial technology but also in amorous technique, since they made earthly women "slaves of the enchantments of the flesh, in accordance with the divine ways of the Children of the Sun."

In this connection Jimmy Guieu states that the angels (extraterrestrials) of the Bible had sexual abilities far superior to those of earthlings.

The descendants of Samirza and earthly women were demigods. They founded a lineage on our planet and served as Instructors to the Atlanteans, the Egyptians and the "peoples living beyond the ocean."

RESURGENCE OF THE *BOOK OF ENOCH?*

All this fits in remarkably well with our best traditions. I believe it evokes the role of those Initiators named Baal, Viracocha and Quetzalcoatl who came from the planet of love: Venus. The *Book of the Children of the Sun* presents a vision of primohistory that is more detailed though similar to that of the *Book of Enoch.* It devotes a hundred and five chapters to the story of the angels, which is hurried over in nine lines in the Bible.

Jika, the author of the saga, the last of the demigods and "the last of the most ancient ones," relates the adventures of "him who had come from the faraway stars to teach mankind: Samirza":

He did not return to the fertile land of his fathers because he had obtained the love of

126

Ophala, daughter of the master of all the inhabited earth. She gave him a son. He did not bear wings like his glorious father. Samirza, the great initiator of the other race, joined with the daughter of men because she was beautiful. He repudiated the land of the faraway regions of the sky and several of his companions remained with him. He became the master of all the inhabited earth. It was he who built the great pyramid bearing the temple of the sun.

Where was that great pyramid bearing a temple? It was not one of the pyramids in Egypt or China, or one of the structures serving as supports for the temples of Mexico. We must therefore assume that this pyramid, which evokes the style attributed to the Atlanteans, was submerged at the time of the Deluge.

For the Deluge is mentioned in the *Book of the Children of the Sun,* and also the end of our time, which appears in a prophecy.

THE PROPHECY OF JIKA

One day the voice of Jika summoned the Children of the Sun to resignation:

You are going to perish, with our divine ways and our temples and our sacred knowledge. For the earth belongs to the perverse race and its accursed sons, and their abominations will shake the stars in the age of shadows. But do not be afraid: their decline will come at the appointed time, and the Children of Light will prepare the return of the the Children of the Gods.

Then we reached the other part of the world. Then we came to the beautiful and fertile expanses where the men of the perverse race had built great cities. Their ways were still divine.

I built no house on the faraway soil. I reached, beyond the ocean, a royal city with golden gates. There I established my residence. There I lived among the sages of the inferior race. Then great terror came upon part of the earth. The divine kingdoms all sank beneath the furious waves and the world belonged to the Children of Darkness.

In the time when my life reached seven hundred years, the Great Prince came to me and ordered me to leave a son of my race, a son who would be consecrated to our knowledge and know how to read the sacred texts. . . . I, Jika, obeyed [with the daughter of the Great Prince]. . . . I poured the knowledge of my forefathers into the mind of the child born of my blood, disdained by my heart. I corrupted the texts, I did not impart the secrets.

The demigod's account ends with a prophecy that gives us to understand that after the end of the world in about the year 2000, extraterrestrials will return to Earth to begin a new cycle:

I am everlasting. I know and I bear the secret of worlds, and I leave to my descendants the prophecy of the demigod who was through me the Master of Masters. Everything will be thus for the terror of the world in times to come, times of calamities, before my brothers the gods, sons of the Sun King, approach the soil in upheaval. . . . Incredible fortunes will come from the bosom of the waters. Nature will be pillaged. The sick will be treated at the bottom of abysses, where vast regions of absolute silence will save those tormented by delirium of the mind. . . .

God will be violated in his prodigious power, despite distances coming closer together in space. And whole peoples will be submerged by enormous cataracts.

However, before the men of tomorrow see the infernal chasm opening in front of them, before they also enter into legend, traces of the first superior human races will be found in their slightest details and studied in the light of day.

The waters, the earth and the mountains will yield up the secret of the ancient races and the history of a single monarch: Jika, son of the gods. . . .

Seek toward the heart of the oceans and seas, under the sand of the arid lands, in the deep belly of the mountains, under the world's highest pyramids. . . .

SEEK THE THRONE OF THE GODS

One final point: the throne of the demigods may be discovered at the bottom of an ocean.

Jimmy Guieu's *Le Livre du Paranormal* contains the complete text of the saga bequeathed through the generations to Lysianne Delsol, who may be a descendant of Jika.

"I suppose," she says, "that the prophecy has been made firmer by many translations. The last one, from Spanish into French, was done in about 1830 by Smail Ben Hassan, a Moslem scholar."

She has written two books on the saga and the prophecy: *La Terre des Dieux* and *Le Dernier Soir du Monde*. They have not yet been published, which is regrettable.

I will leave it to my readers to form their own judgment of these accounts, which I have published with the permission of Lysianne Delsol and Jimmy Guieu. I felt that this fragmentary publication would fit naturally into the context of the great adventure being experienced by mankind at the end of the twentieth century: the announcement of the end of an age, the premonitions of "maverick" archaeologists and the discovery of primohistoric documents, crowned by Dr. Cabrera's stones.

But it is also important to take note of the strange correlations that, in the Bible, the *Book of Enoch* and the *Saga of Samirza Rucatl,* give the certainty that the first earthly civilization was brought by the people of the stars, a view corroborated by modern archaeological discoveries and the fact that governments are now examining the prodigious problem of UFOs without preconceptions.

THE SIERRA OF SILENCE

If those preoccupied with mysteries of the sky were to take an interest in phenomena that are truly valid and worthy of investigation, they would be both astounded and overjoyed. But unfortunately their attention is too often focused on unacceptable cases and testimony whose contradictions and implausibility do great harm to the whole subject.

Harry de la Peña, an engineer at Torreon, in the state of Coahuila, Mexico, has little interest in reports from policemen, motorists and railroad gatekeepers, but he listens eagerly when anyone speaks of the Sierra del Silencio, for strange things happen in that sierra, which belongs to the Mopimi Desert in Coahuila, at about 26°45′ north latitude and 103°40′ west longitude.

Although he is not entirely sure of it, Harry de la

Peña believes that the Sierra of Silence may well be the base chosen by space people for visiting Earth. This opinion is based on assumptions and facts he has brought to my attention through the kind efforts of Mrs. G., my collaborator in Mexico City.

Here is a portion of a letter from the Cultural Center of the Laguna de Torreon to Professor Adolfo Orozco Torres of the Geophysical Institute of the University of Mexico City:

The place to which we refer is northwest of the village of Ceballos, State of Durango, and covers an area that has been explored from San Jose del Central and Mohovano to the twenty-seventh parallel, including the junction of the states of Coahuila, Chihuahua and Durango.

Here are the phenomena observed:

1. In certain parts of this area, propagation of radio waves is difficult and sometimes impossible; hence the name given to the place: the Sierra or Zone of Silence.

We have observed the phenomenon with receivers of high and low frequencies. Possible cause: the existence of an electronic vertex that may be engendered by masses of magnetic iron at certain depths. This is only a hypothesis.

2. Frequent falls of meteorites, of which we have gathered a number of specimens.

3. An abundance of fossils, some of which, according to the physicist Dr. Carlos Graef Fernandez, are more than sixty million years old. They can be picked up from the surface of the ground in sharply defined areas, where crystallized minerals with strange shapes can also be found.

4. Strong and instantaneous concentrations of energy in sporadic form, possibly cosmic or neutron rays.

131

5. Small desert plants with abnormal characteristics probably caused by mutations.

6. On July 11, 1970, at 3:15 A.M., a North American rocket of the Athena type fell in the center of this region, where we had been making observations since April 1966.

AN IDEAL BASE
FOR EXTRATERRESTRIALS

At first sight, this fallen rocket may seem irrelevant, but it actually intensified the mystery, drew the attention of the Mexican government and nearly set off a diplomatic incident, because for several years the United States had been taking too close an interest in the Sierra of Silence.

On March 27, 1970, Werner von Braun had gone to Mexico City in an unsuccessful effort to obtain permission from the Mexican government for construction of an observation base at Ceballos.

Ceballos and Parral y Allende, in Chihuahua, had been described as ideal places for extraterrestrial visitors to land on our planet. Since earthlings determine in advance the best places for their spacecraft to land on the moon, it is logical to assume that if intelligent life exists on other planets, extraterrestrials seek out places on Earth that will give them maximum security.

And an Athena rocket, launched from Utah and supposedly headed for White Sands, New Mexico, had landed at precisely the place where the Americans wanted to establish an observation base. It carried a capsule of radioactive cobalt, which meant that Americans had to recover the dangerous elements and spend a certain amount of time at Ceballos.

"To us," stated a Mexico City newspaper, "it is inconceivable that technicians capable of sending men to the moon, a quarter of a million miles away, should have lost control of a rocket whose course and fuel were minutely calculated by electronic brains. Not only was the rocket turned off course, but it went in nearly the opposite direction and came down seven hundred miles from its destination, at a place where the Americans had been refused permission to go, but where they wanted to go anyway. And why was an *experimental* rocket loaded with radioactive cobalt, if not to justify an intervention for the purpose of decontaminating a whole region?"

And that is exactly what happened. An American military team commanded by a colonel went over the area for twenty-four days, gathering various samples and taking ordinary and infrared photographs. Finally the rocket was located on a plain, near the San Ignacio ranch. It was taken away by the American team, who also took *two hundred thousand tons of earth* and samples from adjacent areas. Trailer trucks were seen several times, with technicians manipulating scientific devices unknown to the Mexicans.

"I can't give you a detailed description of all the strange observations that have been made," Harry de la Peña told me, "but after spending seven years in the Mopimi Desert I can assure you that only professors from the University of Guadalajara and the Technological Institute of the Yucatan have visited that place with no other interest in mind than their studies!"

FANTASTIC TECTITES AND STONES

At almost the same time, in April 1970, the journalist Miguel Angel Ruelas T., of the *Siglo de Torreon,* was investigating the part of the Sierra of Silence where meteorites and tectites are abundant on the surface of the ground. He wrote as follows:

They are fragments of meteorites that fell several centuries ago. I was accompanied by Rosendo Aguilera, who lives in Ceballos, Caledonio Hernandez, a peasant who knows the region like the palm of his hand, the engineer Harry de la Peña and Roberto Contreras Barrios, who holds a degree in physics and astrodynamics. The goal of our investigation was to find out why the Americans were so interested in that area.

It was an adventure full of surprises, beginning with our discovery of the zone of silence in which our radios would not function. Twenty miles farther on, we finally came to "paths" of black stones. From a distance, it was as if we were seeing giant ants on an asphalt road.

We gathered some of the stones, which were too numerous and strangely shaped to be natural. Harry de la Peña found a particularly curious one: it was about an inch long and half an inch in diameter, with a central core that made us think of a piece of cable.

The Aguilera brothers had previously gathered stones with various shapes: a screw head, a knotted steel cable, a high-tension cable perforated from one end to the other, and common tools.

All over the region, animals are subject to strange phenomena, which in earlier centuries would have seemed satanic. They lose their sense of direction, for example. Dogs have fits of terror for no apparent reason. Turtles that venture into the center of the region turn over on their backs, and if they are placed on their feet they roll over again and remain in that position till they die.

EXTRATERRESTRIALS
ARE AT OUR DOOR

Why is the Sierra of Silence a "black hole" in space-time? Why is it an impact point for meteorites? The mystery remains.

According to a Mexico City newspaper, Werner von Braun stated on February 8, 1969, that a Soviet space-craft of the Venus type (probably Venus VI) appeared to be on a collision course with an enormous meteor. Technicians at the Baikonur base made the craft turn aside. A short time later a strange thing occurred: the meteor swerved toward the craft, then returned to its original course and fell at Ceballos.

An investigation made by the Mexicans showed that the meteor had not disintegrated when it entered the earth's atmosphere, but at the point of impact they found a metallic powder that, when examined under a microscope, proved to have a mysterious composition, "like hollow spheres that must have been filled with some sort of gas before they burst."

Every week, always at night, the people of villages in the Mopimi Desert and the Sierra Mojada witness luminous sights that apparently worry them seriously, since they have asked for protection from the federal police.

On the night of March 14, 1973, two brothers, Ruben and Juan Hernandez, had a singular experience. They were working at the Pietra mine at Parral Chi-huahua, when they looked up at the sky and saw some-thing round, like a ball of fire or reddish light, that seemed to be observing them. It came so close that they became frightened and gave the alarm to all the mine personnel by means of the interphone. One of the miners stated that the object remained motionless for a time, as if it were watching the activity at the mine, then started off at incredible speed in the direction of the Sierra of Silence.

It is a commonplace story, of a kind that is reported every day, but luminous UFOs regularly appear in the night sky above the states of Durango, Chihuahua and Coahuila, and *they all disappear in the direction of the Sierra of Silence*. That is why the newspaper *El Mexicano,* of Ciudad Juarez, wrote that "extraterrestrials are at our door."

Is there a base of extraterrestrials in the Sierra of Silence? The Mexicans have no proof of it, but they believe that the Americans know for certain.

THE AGE OF AQUARIUS

It is odd that so many incidents occur in the Torreon-Parral-Monclava triangle in which the Americans are so strongly interested, but that is not all. As I reported in Chapter 23 of my book *The Mysterious Past,* this is a region where significant discoveries have been made: rock carvings of individuals dressed as deep-sea divers or astronauts (between San Pedro de las Colonias and Saltillo) and tombs in which eight-foot giants with blond hair, thought to be of a nonterrestrial race, were buried in the extremely remote past.

Did a cataclysm once occur in the Mopimi Desert, like those that, according to tradition, occurred in Death Valley and the Gobi Desert? One is tempted to think so, since everything seems to indicate that extraterrestrials who had once lived in the sierra knew about the "black hole" and periodically came back to it.

In Mexico many people are convinced that extraterrestrials frequent the Sierra of Silence, that they have contacts with NASA and the Pentagon, and that there will soon be an official meeting between earthlings and space people on Mexican soil. Such a meeting may not take place in the near future—in fact, it seems incredible today—but when it does happen it will perhaps mark the beginning of a new era: the Age of Aquarius.

In any case, since 1973 most of the world's governments have been considering the possibility of a visit from extraterrestrials, and have created special units whose function is to make preparations for it.

CHAPTER 8

Nasca Seen from the Air

SEEN FROM THE AIR, Nasca is fantastic, gigantic and bewildering: an incredibly dense array of drawings and geometric figures stretches across the plain for a distance of sixty miles. Similar markings, known as *pistas* in Spanish, can be seen by pilots and astronauts from Guayaquil to Santiago, all along the Andes.

A Peruvian friend, Anne Bridget B. of Ilo, reports their existence in Chile, where a human figure three hundred feet long has been drawn on the ground, south of Arequipa, in the Moquegua region and in the Tarapaca Desert. They have also been found around Cuzco, near Lake Titicaca and between Santiago and Antofagasta.* And not only *pistas,* representations of people, flowers and animals, but also much more enigmatic

---

* Figures on the ground, intended to be seen from a hilltop or an airplane, are not rare on the globe. In the Glastonbury Valley in England there is a gigantic zodiac on the ground. The winged shape of an ancient temple can be seen on the bank of the Humler, and in the downs of Dorset a large number of white horses, revealed when the

drawings, immense amphitheaters and a Great Wall similar to that of China.

THE SPHINX IN PERU

For reasons that are not entirely clear, Peru has come to be regarded as a kind of special world that has never had the same laws, peoples and civilizations as other countries.

Gold? Yes, of course, there was the gold of the conquistadores, but much less than is commonly thought: only 754 tons between 1493 and 1600. There were the Incas, sun worship, Venusian gods, legends and a fascinating mythology, but there is also something else: a kind of riddle that Peru addressed to all curious minds. It is as if in Peru, as in ancient Egypt, a sphinx asked its question: "What do you think you can discover here?" The answer that should have been given is: "Everything! The secret history of mankind, the mysteries of the cosmos, gold, poisons, religious fanaticism, the archives of earthly people and celestial angels."

Was the world born at Ica, as Dr. Cabrera maintains? Perhaps, but one thing is certain: the oldest known civilization existed in the Andes. And what is even more fantastic, that civilization came from the sky and was brought by extraterrestrials. Evidence for this belief is engraved on the Nascan Desert.

PAUL KOSOK DISCOVERS THE *PISTAS*

In Peru, from Lima to Arequipa, the pampas are vast stretches of sand and loose rock, furrowed during

---

land was cleared, are the work of an ancient people of whom little or nothing is known. There are also several *pistas* on the island of Malta and in the Sahara, and figures of giant men, marked out with stones, in the Mohave Desert of California.

the short rainy season, veritable deserts without grass, birds or animals of any kind, though sometimes an Andes condor flies over those lonely wastelands, attentive to a sight that cannot be seen by human beings.

The *pistas* are found mainly between the Pacific and the Andes, in the pampas of Villacuri, Los Castillos, Huayuri, Colorada and Los Corados. The center of greatest density is between Palpa and Nasca, near the Rio Ingenio. But there are tens of thousands of *pistas* extending into Chile, and in other places where they still remain to be discovered.

The Spanish conquistadores never saw them. The chronicler Francisco Hernandez vaguely mentions great lines drawn on the ground in the Andes, but he speaks only from hearsay.

Professor Paul Kosok of Long Island University and his assistant John Harward were the first to make a systematic study of the *pistas,* in 1939. They were followed nine years later by Maria Reiche, a German archaeologist who published a small illustrated book summarizing her observations. The photographic service of the Peruvian Air Ministry later made a precise survey of the drawings, and one mission of Skylab 2 was to photograph them from very high altitude, but the results have not yet been published.

I first flew over Nasca in 1968 (my second visit was in 1973), filming and photographing the drawings from a low altitude.

A BASE FOR JOURNEYS
INTO ANOTHER WORLD

Pilots from the Pisco military airfield had seen *pistas* for a long time, but without attaching any importance to them.

In Peru as elsewhere, archaeology is an occupation and not a vocation, and because I love that country as a second homeland I deplore the fact that the finest discoveries have been made by foreigners, beginning with Hiram Bingman, the Yale professor who found Machu Picchu.

To fly over the Nasca site, one must first make a stop at the Hotel Paracas, on the seacoast five miles south of Pisco. Facing the hotel, six miles away, is the Candlestick of the Andes, the enigmatic drawing whose two lateral branches end with figures that suggest salamanders or dinosaurs.

In Paracas the traveler can visit a museum containing some famous pottery. (In 1968 this museum had the finest mummies in Peru; in 1974 not one of them was left. Vanished into thin air!) The road that goes down in the direction of Chile leads to the wonders of the pampas.

There is an airport in Pisco, and small planes can be rented for flying over the *pistas*. It is not an easy procedure, however. Anyone who requests an official authorization must deal with red tape, delays and strict regulations, and be accompanied by an officer, since the Pisco airport is a military base. The simplest way is to rent a plane at the base itself. (*See Figure 45.*)

THE CONDOR, THE MAN
AND THE LLAMA

It was a lieutenant who piloted our plane in 1968, and in 1973 it was a captain; they were both excellent technicians for whom flying over the pampa was a routine matter.

In 1968 we were caught by one of the sudden afternoon storms that often arise in the Andes. We had to make a hurried return but we still had time to film, in the Villacuri Pampa, some little-known drawings different from those of Nasca. They represent a man, a llama and a condor with outspread wings. (*See Figure 46.*)

It would have been interesting to go and examine them from close up, but there are no roads across the desert except for the Pan-American Highway, which is very far away, and it would probably have taken several days to locate the site. That was a pity, because those figures belong to a time and civilization different from those of the *pistas*.

Actually it is not clear whether the man is leading a llama or some other animal. Its long, thick tail is reminiscent of the dinosaurs engraved on Dr. Cabrera's stones. Moreover the drawings are not made of white lines against a dark background, as at Nasca, but of dark shapes against a light background. I believe that the ground was "swept" and that dark brown rocks were gathered to form the drawings, which somewhat resemble a bas-relief.

The man is summarily stylized and the animal is even more rudimentary. The condor, or some other kind of bird, forms a more harmonious mass. Around the main figures are other drawings of the same composition, but they are difficult to identify. They may be animals and a form of writing that would deserve the attention of official Peruvian agencies.

I can locate the site very approximately at twenty to twenty-five miles south-southeast of Pisco.

LÍNEAS AND PISTAS IN ALL DIRECTIONS

My aerial survey in 1973 was a more thorough version of my flight in 1968.

In a straight line, Pisco is a hundred miles from the Rio Ingenio, which is the heart of the archaeological area, about an hour from the airfield.

We first flew over Ica, the Pampa Huayura and the small town of Palpa before reaching the deep valley of the Rio Ingenio, a tributary of the Rio Grande. On the north slope of the valley are magnificent *pistas* in the shape of long triangles crossed near their points, as though to announce the site. Their direction—bases west, points east—may be significant if, as Kosok believes, Nasca is a vast astronomical calendar.

The steep south slope leads directly to the Pampa Colorado, which is the area of the drawings. Here, just beyond the valley, begin the straight *líneas* (lines), which go off in all directions, across slopes, ravines and mountains. (*Líneas* are lines resembling long furrows and *pistas* are light surfaces in the shape of runways, either rectangular or triangular, but always ten times longer than wide.)

Even from an airplane four or five thousand feet above the valley, the ends of those *líneas* usually cannot be seen. Many of them, however, end at *pistas,* and a smaller number converge on common centers from which they radiate like the spokes of a wheel or the rays of a sun.

There are thousands and thousands of *líneas* of different lengths, apparently about as wide as a plowman's furrow, going in all possible directions. Without being arbitrary, one cannot give primacy to one *línea* or *pista* rather than another. However, there are particularly long *líneas,* and *pistas* of different widths, from ten feet to more than three hundred.

This tangled profusion, in a system that, in spite of everything, appears to be orderly, is the dominant characteristic that strikes the aerial observer.

A PREHISTORIC LANDING FIELD

I will begin by describing, without analyzing them, the impressions produced by the incredible spectacle of Nasca.

First you notice intersecting *líneas* and *pistas.* Then you have the feeling that you are flying over a landing field, a kind of odd airport where large runways have been built for airliners, and small ones for private planes.

Everything is laid out with an impressive mastery of geometry. The few rounded lines are drawn with a skill that indicates the disorder is only apparent, that though the whole is incomprehensible to us, for brains conditioned differently there is a logic. (*See Figures 47, 48 and 49.*)

The people who laid out Nasca could not have been careless architects; they must have been enlightened mathematicians and talented planners capable of producing designs so large and complex that they could not be seen in their entirety, but had to be laid out on the basis of a precise mental image.

We thus return to the view of Professor Otto Klineberg, who maintains that the Hopis of Arizona are more gifted than other peoples at relativistic physics and abstract mathematics. On this principle, it would seem that our mental processes are not well suited to explaining the mystery of Nasca. The *líneas* and *pistas* can be understood only by the Aymaras and Quichuas, who are descendants of the ancient builders. Perhaps they could give us an explanation, but would we be able to accept it?

THE SPIDER, THE SPIRAL AND THE MONKEY

As we continue flying over Nasca we pass from the *líneas* and *pistas* to the drawings that are like the illustrations of a great page of secret writing. (*See Figures 50 through 59.*)

The first one we see is the hundred-and-fifty-foot spider beside the Pan-American Highway. (*See Figure 56.*) Our plane follows the highway a long time, then turns westward, toward the area where the density of drawings is greatest. We admire perfectly drawn spirals and geometric figures, some of whose sides are formed by *líneas,* others by embankments.

"There's the monkey!" says our pilot, Captain Arboulou.

We have to move quickly to take photographs, film a sequence and see the drawings while the plane describes a curve at an altitude of three hundred feet. Our speed is so great that we must come back to the site several times to examine it and finish our work.

The huge monkey (three hundred feet long) is drawn in action, with his tail curled into a spiral. (*See Figure 53.*) A *línea* cuts across his arms, and two parallel lines, starting from his tail, form a geometric design.

We notice that several of the largest drawings are apparently covered by lines, which would seem to indicate that, contrary to what I believed before (see my book *Forgotten Worlds*), the drawings are older than the lines. The magnificent six-hundred-foot condor, however, has pure, perfect lines on a dark, unbroken background. (*See Figure 58.*)

THE CONDOR, MESSENGER OF THE GODS

According to Edmond Wertenschlag, this "condor" is actually a hummingbird, identifiable by its long beak, but we know that drawings are often prolonged by narrow *pistas.*

In the same area there are more drawings of condors or other birds, one of which has a very long zigzag neck and beak.

The symbolism of the condor in the Andes might help to explain the drawings, since it is the "messenger of the gods." On this hypothesis, the vast array of drawings is a tribute, or rather a message, to superior beings or gods who live in the sky.

Other drawings also pose problems: a parrot (*see Figure 54*), a cat, four-legged birds, reptiles, fish, a chick, a flower (*see Figure 50*), snakes with several heads (*see Figure 51*), objects with indescribable shapes, etc.

Nowhere do we discern a preferred direction or arrangement: the *líneas, pistas,* drawings and geometric designs are intermingled.

The spirals evoke certain stone carvings at the Chavin site, but they are also found in other parts of the world.

Four miles south of Palpa, on the slope of a little hill, are half-effaced drawings of two personages with radiating headdresses. Are they representations of the god Inti (the sun)? We will never know.

Thousands of drawings have become nearly invisible because of erosion. Others have abstract shapes, with multiple Greek borders, square labyrinths and zigzag lines.

CAIRNS AND AMPHITHEATERS IN THE ANDES

On the way back, we fly over a pampa southwest of the Rio Ingenio, where other discoveries increase our perplexity still more.

Líneas burst out in all directions from centers three to five miles apart, located at the points of triangles or on the sides of trapezoids.

On long, white areas are countless dark protuberances more or less in alignment. (*See Figures 60 and 61.*) On small areas there are sometimes only five to fifteen of them. They can also be seen in the foothills of the Andes, where they are called "pockmarks." As we will see later, they are actually cairns (mounds of stones) similar to those made in Europe by the Celts.

These cairns are found all over Peru, even along

roads, but most of them are isolated and were made quite recently. Whole mountainsides in the Andes are covered with strips of cairns thirty to sixty feet wide and more than fifteen hundred feet long.

On the Pampa Maras, fifteen miles northwest of Cuzco, another type of structure arouses our admiration: huge "amphitheaters" six hundred to twelve hundred feet long, hollowed out of the rocky soil. (*See Figure 62.*) They have the form of an arena surrounded by tiered rows of seats, with a flat area on one side, surmounted by an amphitheater. The amphitheater recalls the terraces for growing corn at Ollantaytambo and Machu Picchu, and it may possibly have been used for farming.

The same may be true of the flat areas that look like playing fields, but that explanation cannot be applied to the perfectly flat and circular arenas, thirty to forty feet in diameter, surrounded by seven to twelve rows of seats. They inevitably suggest the idea of open-air sports or combats.

These structures still puzzle archaeologists but it is thought that they were large theaters where the Incas gathered on ritual dates for religious ceremonies or games. The proximity of Cuzco, capital of the Empire, supports this hypothesis.

THE GREAT WALL OF PERU

Our little plane could not, of course, take us into the heart of the Andes or even fly over the first chains of mountains, which were too high and far away. My only photographs of arenas and amphitheaters are those taken by the Johnson-Shippee expedition, which in 1931 drew up an archaeological inventory of Peru, though without discovering the Nasca drawings.

But Johnson did excellent work and, south of Chan Chan, above the Rio Santo, he recognized the Great

Wall of Peru, about forty miles long. It runs across hills and valleys, and at its highest points it is flanked by small detached forts. (*See Figure 63.*) It may have been built by the Incas or the Chimus for the defense of the Empire, but we do not know for certain.

It is made of rough-hewn stones bonded by mud and is seldom more than six or seven feet high, except in ravines. Although it has partially collapsed, it still evokes the heroic age of a civilization much older than we have been led to believe.

In 1967 several caves with beautifully preserved paintings and carvings were found on the shore of Lake Titicaca, near the town of Chinchillapi, ninety miles from Puno. These caves are a veritable Peruvian Montignac-Lascaux, but their paintings, the work of a mysterious people known as the Killas, the "founders of the world," go back only about ten thousand years (as compared to thirteen to twenty thousand for Lascaux and Altamira).

They prove that the horse was known in South America at that time, and other animals that have since disappeared. The men hunted with bows and arrows and, like the later Incas, wore feathered headdresses.

Some of the carvings, particularly in the Kelkatani cave where the "Written Stone" is found, are said to be a form of writing similar to that of the *keros* (wooden vases) identified by the linguist Victoria de la Jara in the Lima Museum in 1962.

THE HISTORY OF NASCA IS WRITTEN SOMEWHERE

For a long time it was thought that the Incas, like the Celts, had no writing and used only a mnemonic system: *quipus,* cords with arithmetically arranged knots that served to record not only figures but also events. (The law codes of Cuzco are said to have been

Gallic writing: the Rom tablets (Rom is a small town in the Deux-Sèvres department of France).

Translation by the linguist Michel Honorrat: "To Jenu Orlimo, lord of the peoples of Aquitaine and Atlantean Gaul and the land of the Pictavi, I say the following: I send this courier from Rom to Tyre," etc.

Part of the Gallic inscription on Solomon's Bronze (or the Iberian Bronze of Botorrita, Saragossa), a proclamation that Solomon is said to have written in Gallo-Hebrew (that is, in Gallic, according to Michel Honorrat), intended for the leaders of Europe, Africa and Asia, between 985 and 945 B.C.

Translation: "Solomon Great Lord, powerful Prince of the West and Asia and Prince Head of State Samuel King of Sidon, country of El-Oela [Tripolitania], lands of Algasi and Gessen, says the following: I send this messenger," etc.

recorded in *quipus* associated with colored signs on wooden tablets.) Then, as science made progress, a Gallic writing and several types of Incan writing were recognized. My friend Michel Honorrat of Marseilles is a great specialist in Gallic writing. Several specimens of it are known, particularly the Rom tablets, which are in the possession of Monsieur Blumereau of Loudun.

The first Incan writing discovered was the kind on colored cloth described by Domingo de Santo Tomas in 1560. It was created by order of the Inca Pachacuti, ninth of the dynasty. Wishing to preserve the history of the Empire, he summoned all the *amautas* (custodians of ancient knowledge) to Cuzco and had them recount the most memorable events, which artists painted on tapestries embellished with gold thread.

These paintings, stored at Cuzco, Pachamac, the temple of Titicaca, Tiahuanaco and Chan Chan, were destroyed by the conquistadores. But Victoria de la Jara believes she has found several copies of them on the wrappings of the Paracas mummies and the short tunics of the noblemen of the Empire.

The Peruvian archaeologist Rafael Larco Hoyle has stated the hypothesis that the "bean" designs on the

Several types of Incan writing have been found, going from the "road sign" style (on wooden goblets called kesos) *to representational figures of this kind, which date from our millennium.*

151

Mochica ceramics may be a system of writing. This is supported by the accounts of the chronicler Fernando de Montesinos.

According to him, the Pre-Incas had writing, but when a plague devastated the Empire about two thousand years ago, a king, acting on the advice of an oracle, forbade all writing, which was held responsible for the epidemic. But initiates, priests or scholars disobeyed the royal edict: they recorded traditions and historic events by means of paintings on tunics, vases and ornamental cloths, and sticks with colored stripes.

Modern archaeological discoveries lead us to think that the mystery of Nasca is probably written on several cloths and *keros,* though unfortunately we are not yet able to decipher the text.

A find by the Peruvian archaeologist Julio C. Tello may be related to the unknown people who made the *pistas.* On the Paracas Peninsula, near Pisco, he discovered several large cemeteries where bodies, all male, were buried in the fetal position. In one cemetery there were *fardos* (sacks used for enveloping mummies) made of cloths so precious and so well ornamented that they had obviously served as shrouds for high dignitaries: priests, princes, kings or gods. But no ruins of a city or temple that could justify the existence of that quasiroyal necropolis have been found in the vicinity of Paracas. Tello therefore believes that "this city of the dead was the final resting place of illustrious men who lived and reigned in other places."

According to Thor Heyerdahl, in his book *Aku-Aku,* perfectly preserved mummies of tall, bearded white men with red or brown hair were found at Paracas. Near them were carvings of boat centerboards. This may mean that the Paracas necropolis was intended for those Initiators or "gods" who came to bring teachings to the Pre-Incas.

At an unspecified place in Peru, Dr. George Hunt Williamson discovered two hundred graves with naked bodies in them. Some of the skulls had a large opening in the forehead—a third eye—whose periosteum showed that it had never been closed. Williamson believed that the site was the necropolis of a long-vanished people whose existence had been forgotten by history. (Reported by *Religion Soleil Inca,* Paris.)

It is significant that the two important sites nearest to Paracas are Ocucaje, where Dr. Cabrera discovered his Primohistoric Library, and the enigmatic pampa where the *pistas* and drawings are found, as well as large amounts of broken pottery, which has traditionally expressed the idea of death or vanished ancestors.

The Paracas cemeteries appear to be more recent than the engraved stones and the *pistas,* but they may indicate that the Incas of Pachamac and Cuzco wanted to be near a very ancient sacred place of which they had only a vague memory.

A LIBRARY OF
TEN THOUSAND VOLUMES

In trying to clarify the mystery of Nasca and the Ica stones, it is useful to make a comparison with what was recently discovered east of Arequipa, in a desolate valley flanked by the volcanoes Ampago, Misti and Cachani.

An international archaeological mission, working from airplanes, counted about ten thousand smooth basalt blocks on which there were more than thirty thousand engravings and paintings depicting animals (birds, snakes, jaguars, etc.) and human beings surrounded by abstract signs, wavy lines and cosmographies that imply precise astronomical knowledge.*

---

* Near Arequipa, the archaeologist Eloy Linares Malaga has discovered many sites, some of them at least eight thousand years old. At Querulpa, Chico and Huacarama there are beautiful paintings whose dominant colors are red, white and yellow. Carvings, and perhaps a form of writing, appear on rocks at the place known as Toro Muerte, three hours on foot from Ciudad Blanca. About thirty similar sites have been found in the department of Arequipa.

These rock carvings and paintings have been photographed from the air but, to the best of my knowledge, no one has yet examined them in detail from close up.

It is thought that this gigantic stone library, spread over an area of nearly four thousand square miles, may record the major events of an unknown people who were perhaps foreign to the empire of the Incas. Here again, the abstract signs, wavy lines and incomprehensible designs may be a system of writing whose deciphering might shed light on the fabulous history of Peru.

I have now described, with a few comments, how Nasca appeared to me from the air during flights over it in 1968 and 1973. Examination of it on the ground was to bring unexpected discoveries.

CHAPTER 9

Nasca Seen from the Ground

THE CANDLESTICK OR TRIDENT of the Andes,* which belongs to the system of mysterious drawings, has the unusual feature of being dug into the sand of a great dune.

EXACT MEASUREMENTS OF THE TRIDENT

My visit in 1973 enabled me to correct the measurements usually given for the famous "Candlestick." Its length is six hundred feet. The crosspiece that supposedly supports the two vertical branches is three

---

* I have become accustomed to referring to it as the Candlestick of the Andes, but it is also known as the Three Crosses and the Trident of the Andes. The last is the most fitting name, since the monument has nothing to do with a method of light or the Christian religion.

hundred and twenty-eight feet from the top. The width of the central branch is seventeen feet between the two inner edges, or twenty feet between the centers of the two ridges. Its depth varies, but averages a little less than two feet.

The orientation of the Trident is northwest-southeast. In a straight line, it is about six miles from the Paracas Hotel. Overland (which is a difficult way of reaching it) the distance is at least double.

The Trident must be placed in the same category as the *pistas,* since it is a mysterious drawing, which can be seen from the air but is also perfectly visible from the ground, on the large hill of the peninsula, or from the sea, at a distance of about a quarter of a mile. (*See Figure 64.*) But at the actual site it is impossible to view the drawing as a whole: one sees only straight grooves that give no idea of the overall design.

The purpose of the Trident is not known; neither is the meaning of the figures surmounting the three branches, which are certainly not the branches of a candlestick.

The hypothesis of a tree of life has been suggested. That is not unreasonable but, for my part, I clearly see a stylized saurian on the left branch.

THREE SANCTUARIES:
PARACAS, ICA, TIAHUANACO

Prolonged southward, the axis of the Trident extends toward Ica, where Dr. Cabrera discovered his stones, then toward Lake Titicaca and Tiahuanaco, sanctuary of the Pre-Inca Empire.

Is this merely a coincidence, or is it the result of deliberate calculation? I do not dare give a definite answer, but it is remarkable that the three points indicated by the Trident—Paracas, Ica, Tiahuanaco—are on a single line and correspond to the places where the three secret sanctuaries of the Andes are located:

—Paracas: a cemetery intended for male, white, bearded, red-haired aliens of whom we know absolutely nothing.

—Nasca: a crypt where the Superior Ancestors buried the unknown history of mankind (Dr. Cabrera's stones).

—Tiahuanaco: an enigmatic temple-city where the Gate of the Sun bears carvings of strange machines and four-fingered men who, like the thumbless Superior Ancestors of Dr. Cabrera's stones, do not belong to our race.

Truly a strange coincidence, if we add the Nascan Desert, just at the edge of the line, with thousands of *pistas* going in all directions, but mainly northwest-southeast, and the Temple of the Sun on the most sacred island in Lake Titicaca, where, according to one tradition, Orejona, the mother of mankind, landed in a spacecraft "brighter than the sun." Especially since Orejona had four-fingered hands and a skull that is elongated in the same way as the giant skulls found at Tiahuanaco (now on display in a La Paz museum).

This fantastic mystery irresistibly evokes a race of superior beings who did not originate on our planet. Elementary logic requires us to consider the hypothesis of a message from either another planet or a people who vanished thousands of years ago. On that assumption, the Trident of the Andes is a marker intended to orient the research of enlightened archaeologists.

MEMORY CHROMOSOMES AND DRAWINGS

In the past there were certainly extraordinary events that made a deep impression on the ancient inhabitants of the Andes and left lasting traces in their memory chromosomes. It is not by chance that, on the mountains along the road from Lima to Paramas, across a desert of sand and stones, there are inscriptions that are quite recent but give a foretaste of the Nasca markings. Circles, family names, political slogans, and so on, often several hundred yards long, convey a message that is commonplace but rather typical of Peru and Bolivia.

The letters and signs are sometimes formed by rows of stones and sometimes by an Andes plant, the *ichu*, whose roots do not become fixed in the ground. (*See Figure 65.*) They are laid out with a rigorous precision of line and spacing that shows the great mathematical ability of the people who make them.

It is likely that no other people in the world are capable of composing such lines of writing with such perfection. In the depths of their subconscious the inhabitants of the Andes still have a sense of geometry and the technique of transmitting ideas inherited from the Incas—and, further back in time, from ancestors who are not those of the European West.

ON THE PAMPA

Paracas is a hundred and thirty miles from the little town of Nasca, lost in the desolate pampas. The Pan-American Highway is a rather good road as far as Ica, but much less useful beyond that point.

On the outskirts of Nasca the river of that same name is only a shallow, muddy stream, and the town itself is far from enticing. It has one dreary main street and smaller side streets that do not tempt one to stroll along them. But the Hotel Turista, built by the government, is quite pleasant. The rooms have minimal lighting and cold showers, meals are plain but acceptable, prices are modest. After a trip across the arid pampas, the Hotel Turista is an oasis of coolness, relaxation and flowers, even though mosquitoes put in an unwelcome appearance in the evening. (*See Figure 66.*)

Despite the name of the hotel, there are almost never any tourists in it. Guided tours do not venture into the region because it has no convenient public transportation. To go from Lima to Nasca, the best procedure is to rent a car, in good condition if possible, with a driver capable of making repairs along the way. A minimum of four days should be allowed for making the trip and exploring the pampa. It is worth noting that there are a few interesting Incan ruins at the western edge of the town.

OBSERVATION FROM A HILL

The first lines are about ten miles from the town, in the direction of Palpa, on either side of the Pan-American Highway. Their relief is accentuated at sunrise and sunset, and discernible if one looks down on them from even a small height. The large *pistas* can be seen from the embankment of the road, but not the drawings. They are invisible beyond a distance of sixty to a hundred feet. In other words, one must stand inside a drawing to see its lines within a radius of about a hundred feet for those parallel or nearly parallel to the line of sight, and only about sixty feet for those at a greater angle to it.

The average altitude of the pampa is sixteen hundred feet, but the Andes lie to the east, with peaks from six to ten thousand feet high.

At kilometer marker 425, to the left of the highway coming from Nasca, four hills, the largest of which is only sixty feet high, provide observation posts that proved to be useful to us. From there the pampa marked by *pistas* and *líneas* extends northward to the Corrados Hills, which border on the Rio Ingenio, westward in a fan-shaped expanse, and eastward in a strip about three miles wide where drawings abound. They are even more numerous in the fan-shaped area, but they are also more widely scattered, so prospecting is easier to the left of the highway, coming from Lima. It was mainly here that we did our research during the four days we spent on the pampa.

Walking is very difficult and, in case of emergency, it would be useless to expect to find any shade or water. The pampa is a veritable Sahara, crossed here and there by little ravines in which a trickle of water flows during the short rainy season (actually, it almost never rains), but this desert is covered with loose stones whose size varies from that of a marble to that of a basketball.

From the top of one hill we saw a *línea* that extended toward the northwest, crossed the highway and ended at a drawing that we were never able to find. Three times our little group—Edmond Wertenschlag, Alain Elias, Emilio the Inca, my wife Yvette and I— followed the *línea* more than a mile toward the drawing, which from the top of the hill seemed to have the shape of a gigantic figure 4, and three times we failed to find it.

That was our first surprise: seen from an airplane, that 4 is absolutely perfect; from a hilltop a mile away, it is clearly discernible; at its actual location, it is invisible. As we approached it, it faded into the profusion of stones. It was the only drawing that vanished in this way.

A *PISTA* SEEN FROM CLOSE UP

Two small *pistas* began less than a hundred feet from the foot of the hill. (*See Figure 67.*) Each of them was an elongated triangle with a base of about ten feet and sides that came together half a mile away.

Here, as in nearly all other parts of the pampa, the

substratum is a chalky substance, a powder much finer than the finest beach sand, but nearly as compact as plaster. It is covered by a thin layer of gravel, as well as the countless dark or reddish stones strewn over the ground. The *pistas* are areas that seem to have been cleared of stones and gravel to make the white substratum visible.

In our time the *pistas* have turned gray because of oxidation and the darker matter that has been sprinkled over them by the wind, but the lines of the drawings have remained almost white, as if they were more resistant to change.

KILOMETER MARKER 419

Guided by our friend Alain Elias, who knows the area well, we went in search of drawings. Our first stop was a restaurant located at kilometer marker 419 on the Pan-American Highway. Within a half-mile radius of that point we found spirals, the hummingbird, the chick, the parrot and birds so large we were unable to identify them because we could not see them in their entirety.

Pistas and drawings can be seen all along the highway between the Rio Ingenio and the Rio Nasca. I especially recommend the areas around the following kilometer markers: 443, 441, 440, 425, 424, 419, particularly on the left, going from Palpa to Nasca.

For two days we explored the pampa, wandering and sometimes becoming lost in its bleak solitude. Once a drawing has been found, it is very hard to return to it after having left it, because there are almost no landmarks.

Most of the large *pistas* are about a foot deep but their edges have crumbled and are not as straight as they appear to be when seen from the air. They are lighter in color than the surrounding surface, but darker than the *líneas*.

One is struck by the geometric appearance of the *pistas* and drawings as seen from the air; when one examines them on the ground, one is disconcerted and almost disappointed, because their magnificent order and precision are no longer discernible. From the air, the pampa is a gigantic page on which a fantastic message seems to be written; on the ground, it is only a desolate desert stripped of its magic and grandeur. Actually it is not disappointment that one experiences, but a feeling of near-certainty that *the message of Nasca was meant to be read from the air*. (*See Figures 68, 69 and 70.*)

WHITE LINES:
BIRD, MONKEY, SPIRALS

Except for the large *pistas,* the figures are scarcely below the surface of the ground. The lines that form the birds, the parrot, the chick, the spirals, the monkey, etc., are five to six inches wide. They are white, with a faint yellowish tinge, and are lightly drawn with small brown stones that do not impair their clarity.

We studied the parrot (more than a hundred and fifty feet long) for a long time. We were able to identify it by the unusual shape of its beak.

The hummingbird is too large to be recognizable, except to Alain and a few local people familiar with the area.

It is easy to make a line with your foot or hand: you have only to scratch the ground lightly and the white substratum immediately appears.

We took samples of stones without learning anything more than we already knew. The sand is so hard and compact that we had to dig with a sharp stone to take samples of it (*see Figure 71*), which explains the preservation of the lines.

Here and there, piles of stones form cairns, some of which have openings at the top. Local people say that wooden posts were once stuck into those little mounds, but that nearly fifty years ago they were taken away to be used as firewood.

Scattered over the whole area are fragments of red pottery of the same type as the ceramics of Nasca 3 and 4 with multicolored painting, about two thousand years old, according to Professors Rowe and Menzel.

With a certain exaggeration, the number of broken vases (and a few intact ones) has been estimated at two hundred and twenty-five thousand, which would seem to indicate that the pampa was once a vast necropolis, but the borings made by Dr. Rossel Castro in 1948 revealed only a few bones of small wild animals.

It is unquestionable that the pottery is abundant at the site but we do not know why it was brought there or if it was deposited intact or deliberately broken as a symbol of death. It is decorated with painted designs, exactly like the *huacos* in the museums of Lima and Ica, but it may very well be much more recent than the *pistas*.

THE MASTERPIECE OF
A COLLECTIVE UNCONSCIOUS

As the peace of twilight descends on the almost lunar landscape of Nasca, the shadows of large stones lengthen and the air becomes heavy with an awesome silence. There are no birds in the sky; apparently no animals are willing to live in a desert more arid and hostile than the Sahara.

We thought of Easter Island, where at twilight the great shadows of the megaliths and statues seem to come alive and haunt the landscape as though to whisper a legend or murmur an appeal.

At Nasca in the evening the specters of the Great Ancestors are absent or hidden beneath the white sand; the phantoms are invisible, perhaps mute or dead, and suggest no explanation for the great surrounding mystery. Yet here, thousands of years ago, a whole people worked patiently, like industrious ants, on a vast project whose purpose is unknown to us. Did they have a plan, a mission? Who can say? Perhaps, because the pampa was like an immense blackboard on which it was easy to inscribe signs, they felt a need to write a message dictated by their subconscious.

We may imagine masses moved by a collective unconscious foreign to reason* carrying out an obscure geometric task, like spiders weaving their admirable webs. Their work baffles intellectuals too sophisticated to grasp the deep reasons behind the mystery and too heretical to have a right to penetrate it.

There is intelligence in that phantasmagoria, but the silence of the pampa seems to rebuke the profane curiosity of non-Initiates.

THE WORLD'S GREATEST
ARCHAEOLOGICAL ENIGMA

In my opinion the mummies of Paracas, Dr. Cabrera's stones and the Nascan Desert markings constitute the world's greatest archaeological enigma, and certain archaeologists maintain that it is the most important message in human history. In any case it is the largest message, in terms of area.

Paul Kosok and Maria Reiche believe that Nasca is an astronomical calendar that was used by ancient

---

* During long flights of migratory birds the whole flock sometimes changes direction instantaneously, as if it were a single being with a single conscious or unconscious mind.

peoples for determining the dates of equinoxes and eclipses, the best times for sowing, and so on. The astronomer Gerald S. Hawkins also believes it is an astronomical calendar, and estimates that it was made between 100 B.C. and 100 A.D.

These hypotheses are unconvincing, since the lines are oriented in too many directions and lie in a desert where no farming has been possible for thousands of years.

A great cemetery? Why should it be so far away from any city or town?

No excavations have been made at the site, except by the inevitable treasure hunters, who have all come away empty-handed, but large stones with carvings on them have been found in two places. One of them depicts a snake's head and a human head of the kind seen on Incan textiles and pottery. It is red, and on the pampa it could be seen from a great distance, especially when the sun's rays struck it obliquely. It was placed upright in 1946; then some *huaqueros* toppled it, so, to preserve it, it was taken away and put in a museum, where it will surely be stolen.

Other stones have circles painted on them.

THE MOUND BUILDERS

It is interesting to compare the mystery of Nasca with that of the ancient mounds in Ohio, Illinois, Mississippi and Wisconsin. (*See Figure 72.*)

At Nasca a people had the idea of making immense *pistas*; in the United States another people built mounds in the shape of geometric figures and animals: snakes, bears, otters, elks, buffaloes, foxes, wolverines, lizards and sometimes human beings. Very little is known about that people, referred to simply as the Mound Builders.

According to a tradition I consider more reliable than official views on the subject, these mounds were built by people of an unknown race who came from "the other side of the ocean," that is, from Europe, and their civilization was destroyed by native Americans.

This tradition is solidly based. Old Irish manuscripts state that thirty-seven hundred years ago the Tuatha de Danann, who came from "the land of mounds" and the "islands of the West," brought their civilization to Ireland. They were of a divine race, and before returning to their country "beyond the ocean and the islands of mist" (Nova Scotia, Prince Edward Island, Anticosti Island), they built mounds and pyramidal monuments similar to those in Mexico. The Tuatha de Danann were ancient Europeans who emigrated to America and then came back to "the land of the first fathers," as they themselves attested, and as the Popul Vuh affirms.

In his poem "The Prairies" William Cullen Bryant writes about the Mound Builders as follows:

Are they here—
The dead of other days?—and did the dust
Of these fair solitudes once stir with life
And burn with passion? Let the mighty mounds
That overlook the rivers, or that rise
In the dim forest crowded with old oaks,
Answer. A race, that long has passed away,
Built them;—a disciplined and populous race
Heaped, with long toil, the earth, while yet the Greek
Was hewing the Pentelicus to forms
Of symmetry, and rearing on its rock
The glittering Parthenon.

. . .

The red man came—
The roaming hunter tribes, warlike and fierce,
And the mound-builders vanished from the earth.

The Mound Builders have been called Adenas by some prehistorians but they were actually Pre-Celts who emigrated to America shortly after the Deluge, eight to ten thousand years ago. Their earthworks seem to have been intended for religious and funereal rites. Conventional archaeology maintains that they lived just before the beginning of the Christian era, but I believe they were much earlier.

Even though they used quite different techniques, perhaps dictated by the nature of the soil (clay in the United States, a "blackboard" with a white substratum in Peru), the Mound Builders may bear a certain relation to the geometric draftsmen of Nasca.

MONUMENTS OF UNKNOWN ORIGIN

The idea of this relation is strengthened by many observations that have been made in America and Europe: the white drawings on a clay background in the Dorsetshire hills; the "giants" outlined by ditches in England and Peru; the geometric alignments of stones in Carnac, France, whose menhirs are probably the archaic phallus; the artificial duck-shaped ponds in Canada, located on routes used by migrating ducks (*see Figure 73*); the mounds and "pyramids" in Brittany, the United States, Peru and Patagonia; the vitrified forts of Scotland and France; the "pockmarks" of the Andes; etc.

Although their techniques are different, these monuments show a gigantism that presupposes a single idea, and a common denominator: an unknown race of builders.

Some authors, such as the Peruvian Manuel Scorza, have not hesitated to write that these mysterious works were left on our planet by extraterrestrials. Moreover, the Nasca *pistas* have been compared to the shiny streaks, about fifteen hundred miles long and five to ten miles wide, observed on the moon. They generally begin at the edges of lunar basins and cross valleys, mountains, plains and crevasses *in straight lines*.

REALITY OR FANTASY?

Stories of Initiators who came from another planet (probably Venus) have a factual basis, or at least many people think so. Starting from this idea, eager seekers of wonders have uncritically embraced illusions and premature phantasms that, at best, will acquire substance only in a conjectural future.

The question of interplanetary relations deserves great attention for the simple reason that, although UFOs are nearly always meteorites, weather balloons, earthly emissions, clouds of electrons from the sun or the moon, or perhaps experimental craft being tested by a power whose capabilities are unsuspected, we cannot rule out the possibility that uninhabited extraterrestrial spacecraft sometimes appear in our sky, either as observation posts or as messages whose meaning we do not understand.

Unfortunately, study of the phenomenon is made difficult, not by the policies of governmental and scientific authorities, but by the delusions of ordinary people who mistake their desires for reality. As a result, it is all but impossible to tell whether a report is true or false, whether it corresponds to a real sighting, a phantasm or a creative thought materialized by a medium, and whether what seems to be a hallucination may not belong to a different universe-system and be as real as jet aircraft and weather satellites.

I have stated the hypothesis that the Nascan Desert markings were the work of an intelligent, cultivated people controlled by extraterrestrial minds or moved by a fantastic collective unconscious. For the same reasons, the masses of people who see flying saucers may be unconscious agents, mediums, of an extraterrestrial superior power that sometimes gives them a single soul and clairvoyant qualities that have little chance of being accepted and understood by rationalists.*

But how are we to distinguish genuine clairvoyants from charlatans, people who are simply mistaken from those who are *determined* to see flying saucers in order to justify their own existence?

Is television reception bad? Flying saucers are the cause! Is there an earthquake somewhere? Flying saucers! A mysterious crime is committed, a scientist disappears, a meteorite strikes the earth, a B-52 crashes somewhere with a nuclear bomb aboard—extraterrestrials are at work again!

Since this attitude is rampant, it is not surprising that, with the increasing fame of the pampa and town of Nasca, they have become favored locations for sightings of UFOs, flying saucers, Martians and other little green men who have come to take a look at our planet.

A WONDROUS TRANSISTOR

I will not be so rash as to guarantee the accuracy of the following stories that belong, if not to the history of Nasca, at least to its legend.

In 1972 Will Roczinsky, a Polish television reporter, went to Los Angeles and from there to Peru, accompanied by a Swedish archaeologist. They flew over the

---

* A rationalist is a limited, underdeveloped and degenerate individual who nevertheless is clever enough to upgrade himself by appealing to the abusive theory of the criterion of reason.

It is undeniable that our reason is circumscribed and imperfect, and often deceives us. A rationalist is therefore limited by his reason and his senses, cut off from the development of ideas and new forms of thought, and degenerate because, more than anyone else, he has lost his powers of extrasensory perception that, allied with the powers of reason, would make him better able to grasp truth.

pistas and, near the town of Nasca, they saw a flying saucer. Roczinsky took the plane back to Pisco. He then went by car to the place where he had seen the flying saucer. Lying on the ground he saw a "pale, bald being with very long teeth," and he filmed his strange discovery.

At this point I will mention some facts that cast doubt on the story. With very rare exceptions, the small planes that can be rented at Pisco are available only in the afternoon and make sightseeing flights over the pampa only between 3:30 and 5:30 P.M. They *never* go to Nasca and they fly only about five miles beyond the Rio Ingenio. Their cruising radius limits the area they can cover. Even assuming that Roczinsky flew back to Pisco at top speed and drove off in a car immediately, darkness would have fallen by the time he reached Palpa, thirty miles from Nasca, and he would therefore not have had enough light to film anything.

In any case, according to the story, on the dead "being" Roczinsky found "a polyester tetrahedron containing a transistor made of titanium oxide [*sic*]" that functioned on a frequency of four hundred megahertz. With it he tried to make contact with space people. He received some signals from Vega but was unable to achieve any real communication. One day, discouraged, he threw the tetrahedron and its contents into the Pacific.

On November 11, 1972, Roczinsky was killed (at the age of forty-two) in a car accident on the highway from San Diego to Los Angeles. Photographs, tapes and eleven reels of film were taken from his wrecked car. They formed a fantastic reportage made of fragments, interviews and film sequences. The magazine *Das Aktuelle Forum* put the pieces together and invented a unity for them.

No credence can be given to this implausible story in which, as in all others of the ilk, the concrete evidence has vanished as though by magic.

PERU, THE LAND OF UFOs

On February 3, 1972, two respectable citizens of the town of Nasca (they are feed dealers) were crossing the Pampa Carbonera when they saw a flying saucer on the ground. Near it was "a man of average height, wearing green clothes under a transparent space suit."

Tito Rojas and Adolfo Penafiel went to the place to greet the strange visitor, but as soon as he saw them, he stopped his inspection of the pampa and took off. The saucer rose into the air with a shrill, metallic whine, a sound familiar to the people who live in the area, which would seem to indicate that the pampa is a landing field for extraterrestrials.

Flying saucers are now seen all over Peru. The "experts" counted two hundred and fourteen "reliable" sightings in 1973. In more than ninety percent of them, the saucers were piloted by beings who seemed human except for their size and the color of their skin. In eighteen cases the pilots appeared to be robots.

There are a number of doubtful points in these stories, but many Peruvians are convinced that their country was predestined for visits from extraterrestrials because on the wrappings of the Paracas mummies and in rock carvings and the bas-reliefs of monuments there are personages wearing what seem to be space suits.

EXTRATERRESTRIALS CANNOT
BE RULED OUT

To explain Nasca, we must take account of the fact that the drawings were made to be seen from the air and not from the ground. They were intended for real or supposed observers coming from above.

In the Middle Ages one would have thought of God, gods or angels. Those entities are now outmoded and twentieth-century man is obliged to replace them with aviators or travelers from another planet, that is, extraterrestrials.

This is an idea that shocks many timorous minds but it cannot be rejected without ruling out the only reasonable explanation. The explanation of a fantastic phenomenon is necessarily fantastic.

The reason for the permanence of the white lines is already known. The climate of Nasca is terribly dry and the sun shines more than ten months out of the year. The stones store intense heat, which causes the formation of a nearly constant layer of hot air, about a foot thick, that protects the drawings from the wind.

It was once thought that Nasca was a vast burial ground because of the countless fragments of broken pottery scattered over the site, and that the drawings were emblems of various tribes. But no human bones have been found there. And what meaning are we to give to the drawings?

The makers of the *pistas* obviously had a keen sense of geometry because the deviations observed in the lines do not exceed ten seconds of arc, which is insignificant over such great distances. The layout could not be done better in our own time.

It has often been said that the precision of Nasca can be explained only on the assumption that the work was directed by someone watching from either a mountaintop or some sort of craft flying above the pampa. This is an idea that immediately comes to mind, but I believe that the accuracy of the layout can be attributed to the special mental structures of the people who planned it.

It should be noted that *pistas* are almost never found near significant rises in the ground.

Several newspaper articles have stated that miniature reproductions were discovered near all the giant drawings. There is no basis for that assertion.

Part of the problem, at least, is solved: the Nasca drawings are the work of a remarkably civilized people with an amazing grasp of geometry who lived in the remote past, before the Incas. They were probably of the same race as the builders of the Gate of the Sun in Bolivia, and the solar observatories from which they were able to study the explosion of the nova that created the Gum nebula.

It is logical to assume that those Pre-Incas either were in contact with the Initiators mentioned by tradition or had preserved a memory of them. Thousands of years ago, in obedience to direct orders from the Initiators or for the purpose of perpetuating the teachings they had received in the past, they engraved the rudiments of the ancient knowledge preserved on Dr. Cabrera's stones and created the vast page of writing that is Nasca.

SCIENTISTS AND VISITS FROM EXTRATERRESTRIALS

The possibility of visits from extraterrestrials is accepted by many physicists and astronomers.

Pierre Guérin, research director of the Paris Astrophysical Institute, does not believe that such visits have taken place, but in his book *Planètes et Satellites* he writes, "If, in other planetary systems, there are extraterrestrials who have developed an intelligent civilization, there is every likelihood that those beings, the product of a much longer process of biological evolution than the one that led to man, study the universe by means of techniques completely unknown to us and perhaps, in certain cases, fundamentally inaccessible to our reason."

The magazine *La Recherche,* in an article titled "Extraterrestrials Now Interest Astrophysicists," estimates that five percent of all stars have at least one inhabitable planet.

Sebastian von Hoerner gives the following statistics concerning the longevity of technological civilizations: five percent destroy all life on their planet within a hundred years; sixty percent disappear within thirty years if they have a superior technology; fifteen percent degenerate after thirty thousand years of existence; twenty percent lose all technological interest after ten thousand years.

Carl Sagan has stated the hypothesis that a million advanced civilizations exist in our galaxy.

G. V. Forster estimates that if extraterrestrials are capable of traveling ten light-years in space, our solar system has probably received visitors during its five billion years of existence. The number of visits would be about four hundred if the spacecraft of highly advanced civilizations had a range of fifty light-years.

Conley Powell has calculated that the technology required for such a feat should be within the scope of several supercivilizations in the cosmos.

A MOTHER PLANET
IN THE COSMOS

These conjectures lead to a reconsideration of the appearance of life on our planet.

It may not have arisen spontaneously, through the action of amino acids and water, as Oparine and Miller hypothesize; it may have been brought by extraterrestrials from a mother civilization billions of years old.

If so, man himself is an extraterrestrial. This is in accord with ancient traditions, particularly those of the Hindus, whose ancestors are said to have come to Earth "by the path of Aryaman, which begins at a star."

It should be pointed out that few astrophysicists are well versed in mythology and few mythologists know much about astrophysics. I believe that a synthesis of all knowledge in both these disciplines would permit better study of the problem.

The Nasca drawings and the cosmographies of Bolivia and California, combined with the observations and studies of astronomers, form a collection of important elements that enables rational minds to consider it quite possible, if not probable, that extraterrestrial Initiators came to our planet thousands of years ago.

Furthermore, twentieth-century social phenomena not only support the possibility of such an occurence, but explain it in a curious and convincing manner.

GODS WHO CAME FROM THE SKY

During World War II American forces came to New Guinea and other Pacific islands, bringing tractors and bulldozers with which they made long runways lighted by electricity from powerful generators. Then fighter planes and bombers landed on the runways.

To get on good terms with the Papuan natives, the soldiers gave them food, cigarettes, chewing gum, knives and pictures of Rita Hayworth. To the Papuans, it was as if the presents came from the sky, along with the big metal birds.

Then the war moved on and the planes were transferred to other bases. Years went by. The Papuans waited in despair for the return of the big gift-bearing birds. Gradually, with nostalgic yearning for the happy days of the past, and also with the rise of a new generation who had known the wondrous birds only by hearsay, a tradition was born.

"In the old days," said the elders, "men came from the sky and brought gifts."

Little by little, a desire-image took root in the minds of the Papuans. They had noticed that in order to make the big metal birds come, certain rites had to be performed: clearing and leveling the land, making bright lights that evidently had the purpose of attracting travelers from the sky.

Within twenty years the visitors and their fantastic flying machines had become gods who dispensed all sorts of blessings. The Papuans decided that perhaps they could make them come back if they revived the rites of clearing land and making bright lights. The runways had long since been devoured by the jungle, but in the areas where they had been, and also in other places, the Papuans cleared and leveled the ground and made big bonfires. They even built effigies of the flying machines and ritually burned them, inventing songs, dances and a whole worship ceremony.

The gods have never returned, but worship will probably be continued for centuries and we may assume that someday the Papuans will have forgotten the original basis of the tradition. Then they will invent a mythology, as the people of the Andes invented one for the anniversary of the appearance of the Gum nebula.

NASCA: AN APPEAL TO THE GODS

The past existence of highly civilized Superior Ancestors in the region of Ica is attested by Dr. Cabrera's eleven thousand stones. Those Initiators, with their advanced knowledge of surgery, geography, physics and astronomy, probably departed or disappeared a short time after their arrival, since they left no lasting monument to their presence, except for teachings that have partially survived in adulterated but conclusive form.

After the departure of the divine Initiators of Ireland (the Tuatha de Danann) and the flying gods of the Papuans (American airmen), the contacted peoples dedicated worship to them, expressed by dolmens and menhirs in Europe, and runway fires in the Pacific.

Similarly, there is reason to believe that the ancient

We found stones in the homes of all the inhabitants of Ocucaje.

Emile Fradin's triumphant smile. Glozel has been recognized as genuine by Danish, Norwegian and Swedish scientists. The humble French peasant has vanquished such pundits of prehistory as Capitan, Peyroni and Breuil.

Photo Robert Charroux

The meaning of this drawing remains uncertain. It may symbolize the coming of helmeted flying men (astronauts), carried by a large bird (aircraft or some other type of flying machine).

A kiang, an onager or a wild horse?

The horse lived in America twenty thousand years ago, then became extinct. In the sixteenth century the conquistadores introduced it into Peru and Mexico. This drawing may therefore date from the sixteenth century or later, or it may be more than twenty thousand years old.

A Judeo-Christian myth or a universal one? Eve, Adam and the cat-serpent.

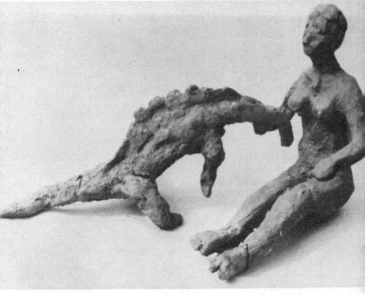

Woman playing with a dinosaur.
Many Acambaro ceramics depict animals that do not belong to our Quaternary era. There are often various species of dinosaurs, some of which seem to have been tamed or domesticated by man. This coexistence of dinosaurs and human beings supports the ideas suggested by Dr. Cabrera's stones.

Pierre Vogel (at the tiller), the geologist Professor Dujardin and the diver Jacques Mayol went to visit the undersea city of the Veyron many times.

The Lady of La Vaulx.

Altar adorned with a sun sign.

Carved stone at La Vaulx.

This is the plane in which we flew over Nasca.
Left to right: Captain Arboulou, pilot, Robert Charroux, Edmond Wertenschlag.

Left: the man and the llama. Right: the condor. Center: partially effaced depictions of animals presumed to be camels.

Photo Servicio Aerofotografico Nacional del Peru

Nasca: an immense landing field that can be seen only from the air.

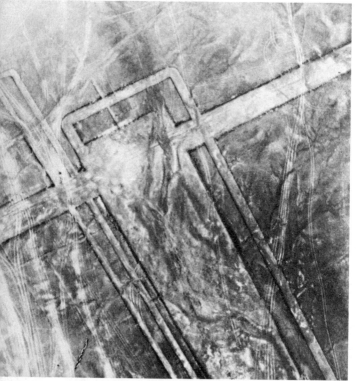

Nasca: The geometry of the lines and pistas *is so perfect that it defies the imagination, and perhaps the technical possibilities, of the twentieth century.*

Facing page, top to bottom: Nasca: the flower, the snake, the mermaid.

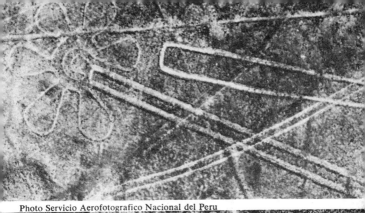

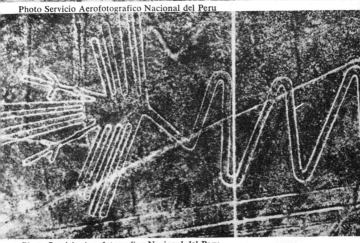

The monkey, three hundred feet long.

The parrot.

The dog.

Facing page: The spider, a hundred and fifty feet long.

Photo Servicio Aerofotografico Nacional del Peru

Two personages with radiating hair or headgear, Pampa Palpa.

The condor with spread wings, six hundred feet long.

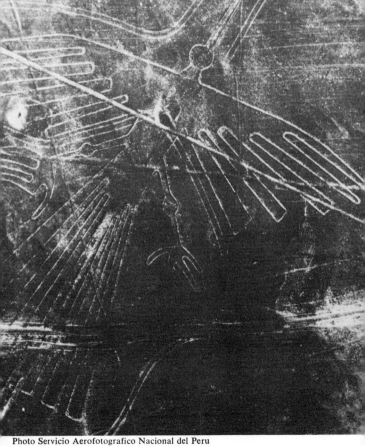

Photo Servicio Aerofotografico Nacional del Peru

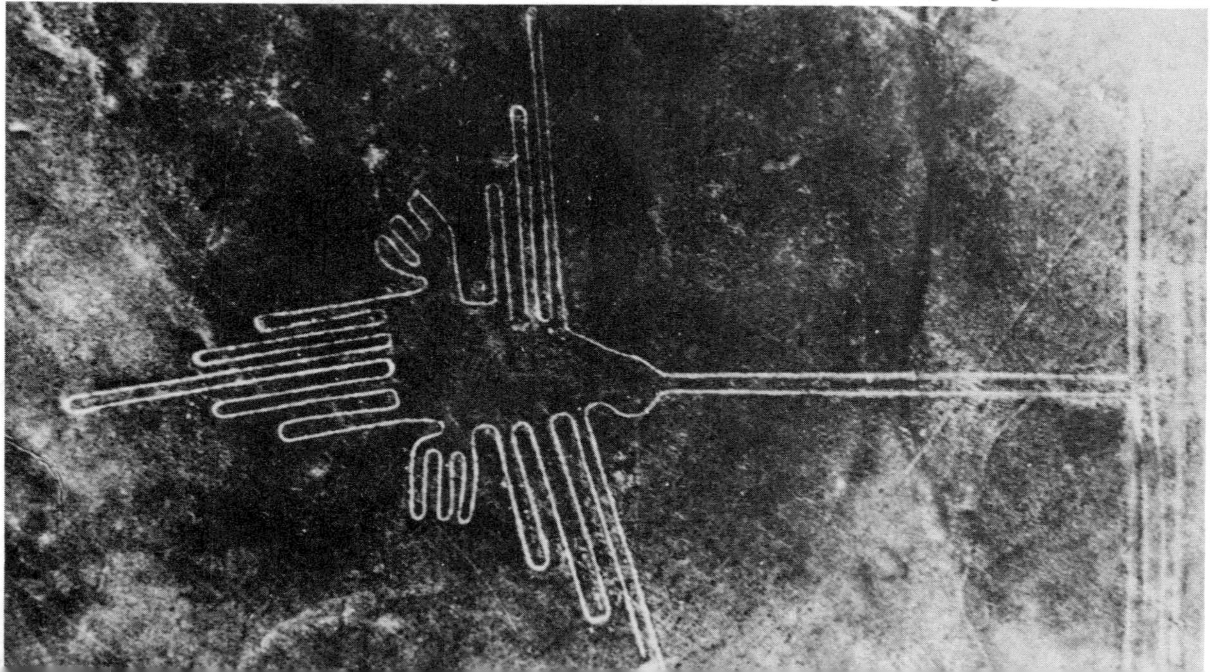

Facing page: the hummingbird.

The mysterious "pockmarks"—perhaps they are tombs—spread over spurs of the foothills.

Amphitheaters discovered in the Pampas Maras, fifteen miles north-west of Cuzco.

Photo Illustration 1932

The Candlestick of the Andes as it was seen in 1974.

The archaeological treasures of Peru are not protected. Vandals in Land-Rovers or on motorcycles ravage the site of the Candlestick. Within a few years they will have done irreparable damage to it.

The Peruvian wall discovered by the Johnson expedition, with the ruins of a village in the foreground.

Photo Robert Charroux

A survival of chromosomal memory? On the mountains between Lima and Paracas the people of the region still make inscriptions whose letters are formed by aligned stones or ichu *plants.*

After our visit to the Nascan Desert: relaxing at the Hotel Turista in Nasca.
Left to right: Yvette Charroux, Francis Mazière, Dr. Cabrero, Edmond Borit, Colonel Omar Chioino Carranza, director of the Peruvian Aeronautical Museum.

From the top of a hill, two small pistas *can be seen against the dark* background *of the plain.*

67, 68

A spiral. When the lines are seen horizontally, they fade away at a distance of a hundred feet.

The edge of this large pista *is sharply defined when seen from the air, but is blurred from close up.*

Here is how the pampa appears from the surface: a stony desert. The drawings fade into the distance so much that it is difficult or impossible to recognize what they represent.

Taking a mineralogical sample.
A línea is only about eight inches wide.

Facing page, top: the Great Serpent, twelve hundred feet long, in Ohio, a vestige of the mysterious mound-building Adenas. Bottom: in Canada the flight paths of migratory ducks are studded with artificial ponds dug in the shape of a duck. Like the Nasca drawings, this one is made to be seen from the air.

Photo Tony Linck

Photo Frank Chalmers

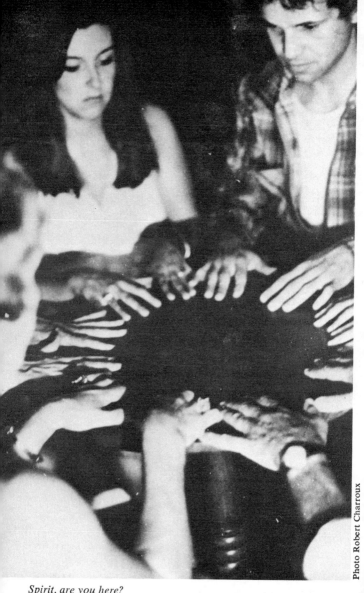

Photo Robert Charroux

Spirit, are you here?
The hands must form an unbroken chain, to let the fluid flow—or perhaps to engender it.

peoples of Bolivia and Peru commemorated the visit of beings of divine blood by traditions concerning Orejona and her Venusian spacecraft and by the carvings on the Gate of the Sun, the Ica engravings and the Nasca drawings. That is probably what a Nasqueño would say if Hispano-Christian civilization had not effaced from his mind the memory of the great events witnessed by his ancestors.

Considered in isolation, Nasca is an impenetrable enigma, but its meaning becomes clear when it is placed in context: the mysterious white, bearded, red-haired individuals sumptuously buried in the Paracas necropolis; the big-headed giants of Tiahuanaco and the four-fingered extraterrestrials carved on the Gate of the Sun; the secret caves of Ocucaje and their scientific revelations; the Trident of the Andes, rising above the sea of the god Poseidon and facing the sky.

According to tradition, Poseidon, god of the ocean, was the king of Atlantis. The symbols of Atlantis were the trident and the seahorse. Is the Trident of the Andes a signature left by Atlanteans who had escaped the destruction of their country?

THE SACRED LINE FROM TIAHUANACO TO PARACAS

There is undoubtedly great significance in the northwest-southeast direction followed by most of the Nasca lines, the axis of the Trident and the incredibly straight line that passes through the Paracas necropolis, the caves where Dr. Cabrera's stones were found, Nasca and the fascinating Gate of the Sun at Tiahuanaco.

The Gate of the Sun is oriented in such a way that the rising sun at the solstice shines through its opening, then passes over it and goes on to light Nasca, Ica and Paracas.

As for the enigmatic Trident, at the other end of the

"sacred line," it is on a hillside with an average slope of thirty-eight degrees, so that its three upper extremities are aimed at the sky in a specific direction.

To what is this symbol of Poseidon pointing? Is it the Land of Mu, which lay on the other side of the Pacific in the remote past? It is difficult to accept this idea if we take account of the slope of the Paracas hills.

It is not by chance that the "sacred line" from Tiahuanaco to Paracas rises abruptly as though to indicate a point in the sky probably related to the Great Ancestors who built the sanctuaries, or in whose memory they were built. And precisely in the direction given, some twenty-five million miles away, Venus the Divine glitters in the evening sky: Venus, the home of Chasca, Viracocha and Orejona, according to tradition, and perhaps also the home of the Initiators of earthly knowledge.

When Venus accompanies Inti, the sun god, describing an arc of a hundred and eighty degrees, the Trident of the Andes points in the direction of Sirius, the Sothis of the Egyptians and the mother of our solar system according to the Dogons of Africa.

Sirius occupies an important place not only in the mythology of ancient peoples, but also in their astronomy.

THE PATH THAT LEADS TO THE STAR

At the Neolithic site of Medzamor, in Soviet Armenia, Russian archaeologists have discovered a veritable factory where eighteen varieties of bronze were manufactured ten thousand years ago.

On the bank of the stream that runs beside the site, E. S. Parsamian of the Burakan Observatory identified three ancient triangular observatories from which, according to calculations that have been made, Neolithic people were able to see the rising of Sirius at about four o'clock in the morning on June 22, 2800 B.C.

It also happens that the first month of the ancient Egyptian year, called Thoth (the Initiator), began with the appearance of the star of Isis: Sirius or Sothis.

Enlightened astronomers may someday tell us if the Gum nebula also lay in that direction, which so strongly interested the scientists of the Andes plateau forty thousand years ago. If so, we may find a singular association of clues that will provide an explanation of the mystery of the Andes.

Another remarkable fact: a line drawn perpendicular to the "sacred line" at its center passes exactly through Cuzco and Sacsahuaman, the sacred city and fortress of the Incas.

There is no defensible reason to oppose the probable truth that emerges from all this: it was in order to pay tribute to the great birds that came from the sky thousands of years ago, and to honor the gods who brought from their home planet the arts of replacing a sick heart, seeing the stars from close up, smelting metals and writing, that the Pre-Incas covered the surface of the Nascan Desert with *pistas* and drawings of flowers, animals and immense birds resembling those of the Initiators.

If the secrets of the telescope and the magnifying glass are related to the Superior Ancestors who came ten to forty thousand years ago, we may assume that the last celestial groups were composed of extraterrestrials from Venus, as tradition maintains. It must be remembered that the gods of the Incas and the ancient Mexicans, like those of the Babylonians and the Phoenicians, were representatives of the planet Venus. From this we may infer that the last gods (extraterrestrials) landed at Nasca five thousand years ago. But before them, ten to forty thousand years ago, other extraterrestrials also came to visit our planet.

On this hypothesis, the drawings of birds at Nasca represented the spacecraft of the gods; the spirals, lines and geometric figures represented their landing installations; the flowers represented an offering; and the animals represented the ritual blood sacrifice that primitive people have always felt they owed to the gods. A form of worship, but also an appeal to the ancient visitors, an invitation for them to return.

The prayers of all peoples, from India to the Americas, from Africa to Greenland, rise toward the stars. A cathedral, an obelisk and the spire of a church or a temple are, in the vertical plane, what the Nasca drawings are in the horizontal plane: the terms of an attempted dialogue between earthlings and the gods of the sky.

In the twentieth century efforts to make contact have necessarily taken a more scientific form, but they are a continuation of a very ancient custom, and an announcement that someday interplanetary travel will again become a reality. There can be no doubt that we will go to visit other peoples in the cosmos, just as they have come to visit us.

CHAPTER 10

❧❧

Apocalyptic Times

WITH REGARD TO EXTRATERRESTRIALS and the possibility of their coming to our planet, I have mentioned Sebastian von Hoerner's theories concerning the duration of technological civilizations and their inevitable accelerating deterioration, in direct relation to the extent of their development.

According to Von Hoerner, five percent of these civilizations destroy all life on their planet within a century, and sixty percent disappear within thirty years if their technology is very highly advanced. It is thus interesting to estimate the stage earthlings have reached, and what fate they are preparing for themselves.

One might think that the scientific progress made since the end of the nineteenth century, and the technological achievements that have followed, have led us to the edge of an abyss into which we will soon fall. That idea could be applied to about a fifth of the world,

181

but not to the underdeveloped nations. We must decide whether the term "civilization" refers to an ethnic group, a nation, a continent or the whole planet.

During the last four thousand years many civilizations have blossomed and disappeared, sometimes without leaving a trace, but most of them have left vestiges with little relation to their brilliance. In Tiahuanaco, Ica, the Ahaggar Mountains, Olmec Yucatán and probably Greenland, almost nothing has survived. In Egypt, Phoenicia, Babylonia, Mohenjo-Daro, Greece and Petra, traces remain, but it seems highly unlikely that those nations and cities will ever return to their former grandeur.

Yet our planet has continued its development; the torch of progress has been passed along in accordance with relatively mysterious historical and geographical factors. We must therefore conclude that while the civilizations of France, Germany, the Soviet Union, Great Britain, Italy, Canada, the United States, etc., are now in full flower and therefore inevitably doomed, other nations, particularly China, are ready to carry on.

In the past ideas and technology were at a relatively low level and their propagation was slow and difficult. In the twentieth century, with the accelerating pace of progress, everything is different. There can be no doubt that first China, then Mexico, Brazil, Islam and Black Africa will reach the technological level of Europe in less than a century.

It is thus in the twenty-first century that Von Hoerner's theory, if it is accurate, will be justified.

THE PUGWASH COMMITTEE

Clear-headed people are haunted by premonitory signs of a coming end of the world. These signs are related to most social, industrial, political, moral and religious activities, and are manifested in the proliferation of murders, robberies and immorality, deadening of the sense of duty, work and good citizenship, protest raised to the rank of a principle (though often justified), frantic pursuit of pleasure, miscarriages of justice, inequality based on criminal racism and outrageous privilege, selfishness, lack of brotherhood, the dictatorship of money, the stultifying effect of the mass media, and the control of advanced technology exercised by politicians and businessmen concerned only with their own personal advantage, with the more or less conscious assistance of scientists.

Some scientists, however—physicists, astrophysicists, sociologists, biologists, chemists, geologists, psychologists, mathematicians, etc—have felt justified anxiety over the fate of our planet.

In 1957 eminent thinkers from all parts of the world, with the exception of China, met at Pugwash, a small town in Nova Scotia, to consider what they could do to save our civilization. These scientists undoubtedly had an admirable ideal; they were disinterested and sought only to be men of goodwill in the service of earthly brotherhood. But it was difficult for them to overcome the world's legitimate suspicion of inventors of explosives, cannons, poison gas and atomic bombs.

Freud believed that God and religion lay at the origin of mankind's deep obsessive neuroses. That may very well have been true in the Middle Ages, but I believe that since the end of the nineteenth century mankind's greatest stress has been generated by fear of science and its human embodiment, who often appears satanic: the scientist.

The old myth of the loss of the earthly paradise and the tree of knowledge of good and evil has reappeared in our time as a solemn and terrible warning. Those who perceive it are horrified by it and are beginning to believe in superior laws, in a universal conscience and morality that cannot be violated with impunity.

By working on the manufacture of the atomic bombs

that struck Hiroshima and Nagasaki, physicists deliberately set out on the path to murder. Those men, whose names are now honored, will be regarded as monsters in the future.

The physicist Leo Szilard, the chemist Linus Pauling (Nobel Peace Prize), the biologist Gregory Pincus, Pope John XXIII, Albert Schweitzer, Konrad Lorenz and Jean Rostand are among the best-known scientists and scholars who have taken a position against nuclear weapons.

In an effort parallel to that of the Pugwash meeting, Jean Rostand, Professor Marois, François de Clermont-Tonnerre and a number of world-famous biologists, with the support of Mrs. Nina Khrushchev, gathered on February 4, 1962, at the Château de la Muette in Paris, and founded the Institute of Life, whose goals I described in my book *One Hundred Thousand Years of Man's Unknown History*.

CHIEF, SORCERER, PRIEST, SCIENTIST

If we want to know where we are going, we must know not only where we are, but also where we have been. Study of our possible future therefore begins with mankind's earliest ages, when our prehistoric ancestors began founding a society.

They quickly learned that their existence was precarious: impossible on an individual level, possible if they formed a group to confront dangers and the problems of survival.

The first organized society was the clan. According to the sociologist Lucien Lévy-Bruhl, a specialist on the subject, for maximum effectiveness the clan had to be composed of about thirty individuals. If it was considerably smaller, it became vulnerable and lacked defensive strength; if it numbered much more than thirty, it risked a shortage of resources in the area it used for hunting and fishing.

It was important for the clan to be governed by the strongest and most intelligent individual: the strongest so that he could impose his decisions, the most intelligent so that he would not be mistaken, since any error on his part might be disastrous to the group.

At an early stage, however, there was a division of power between the strongest person—the chief—and the wisest: a patriarch or a group of elders, with proven knowledge and experience. The patriarch decided which actions the group would carry out, under the command of the chief. They both knew where to find fish and game, how to remove the bark from a tree, make stone tools and choose a campsite.

Then specialization of knowledge brought the beginning of a more complex society. The sorcerer came into being. He knew medicinal plants and the secrets of nature. Imposing his will as the conscious soul of primitive society, he invented a morality, obligations, rites and finally a religion.

Having become a priest, he occupied a position of power beside the chief or king. Sometimes, as in ancient Egypt, the king himself was regarded as a priest.

For thousands of years the priest played the part of an initiator. Then, just as religion had been added to sorcery, science was associated with theology until it finally separated from it when dogma became too flagrantly opposed to experimental laws. From then on, the priest confined himself to his religious functions, with timid incursions into the laboratory, and the scientist accentuated the separation by gradually freeing genuine knowledge from superstition and religious pseudotruths.

The development of modern industry and advanced technology finished the process of bringing the scientist to the top of the social hierarchy. In our time he is the *deus ex machina* of civilization.

DESIRED AND UNDESIRED

We now have such a strong need for the scientist that we think if he were to disappear it might be the end of the world. Unfortunately the world will probably end *because of* the scientist, since the good he brings to mankind always has its bad counterpart.

Twentieth-century people are eager for happiness, but instead of seeking it through patient work and virtue, they demand that it be given to them as quickly as possible by those whose knowledge can work miracles: physicists, chemists, biologists, mathematicians. Puffed up with pride and often unaware of his responsibilities, the scientist, in exchange for money and prestige, works, studies and finally finds what is desired. But his discovery inevitably brings with it something that is not desired.

Doctors are asked for a vaccine or a remedy against a certain disease, but the vaccine or remedy makes the body more vulnerable to other diseases.

Scientists are asked for more rapid means of travel and they invent the automobile, which requires construction of smooth, even roads. This leads to a demand for greater speed, and the demand is eventually met by production of cars that go more than a hundred miles an hour. The final result is slaughter: seventeen thousand killed and three hundred and ninety thousand injured in France each year, including one hundred and fifty thousand who will remain crippled or handicapped the rest of their lives. In the United States the figures for 1968 were fifty-five thousand dead and two million three hundred thousand injured. In that year alone car accidents took as many American lives as the whole Vietnam War.

In the past we burned wood to heat our homes. Then scientists gave us more convenient energy in the form of petroleum products, which are now polluting the air at a disastrous rate. To remedy that pollution, scientists have invented thermonuclear energy. Soon it will heat our homes and run our cars. The air pollution of petroleum fuels will be replaced by radiation that causes leukemia and mutations. People will become sterile or produce children with three eyes and five legs; plant reproduction will be affected in the same monstrous way.

Where will the process end? Will scientists blow up the whole planet? Will that be the final adventure of the "animal endowed with reason," as man has humorously named himself. There is reason to think so, because man's incessant demands and two-edged solutions have created a state of serious social and psychic imbalance.

And scientists, become lucid in spite of themselves, are beginning to realize that if they continue their mad struggle the day will come when they can no longer triumph over nature's inexhaustible forces.

WILL NATURE SAVE ITSELF?

The Pugwash Committee concluded that the civilized world can count on only a few more decades of survival. There is one hope, however, that is far from negligible: scientists may be mistaken. Their predictions are solidly based on facts and figures, but they do not take into account the unknowable Intelligence of the Universe, whose designs are almost entirely beyond the grasp of the human mind.

Pollution, nuclear bombs, overpopulation and aggression against nature are serious dangers but they can be swept away by an enormous earthquake or flood, or a cosmic cataclysm. In the remote past our Superior Ancestors probably experienced situations similar to ours, and nature ended them with drastic remedies, annihilating what was gangrenous. The human race, though decimated, was then able to carry on.

We may hope that when our apocalyptic times reach their critical point, the world's scientists or sages will be able to take the necessary saving measures. Nothing is impossible for man: neither the best nor the worst.

THE GREAT FEAR OF THE YEAR 2000

Fear of a worldwide cataclysm is as old as mankind. And yet, while there have been ends of civilizations, the whole human race has never been irremediably damaged, even by the Deluge.

It is probable that fear of the year 2000 will soon begin raging like a contagious disease, accompanied by ancestral terrors and breaches of trust.

That is what happened just before the year 1000, when all of Christendom expected the end of the world. The Church used its great power to strengthen that belief, which was eminently profitable to it. In cathedrals bishops announced the coming of the time predicted in the Book of Revelation. Priests preached on the same theme to their credulous congregations, whose childish imaginations engendered sinister images of hell and punishment.

Did the clergy believe in those false predictions? We cannot say with certainty, but frightened people, rich and poor, gave a good part of their possessions to the Church in the hope of tilting divine judgment in their favor.

An epidemic of visions and hallucinations added to the disorder. People saw the devil everywhere and felt themselves tormented by him while they worked or slept. The slightest unfortunate incident was attributed to him.

In our time this rash of hallucinations has its counterpart in reports of flying saucers and landings by Martians.

As though to justify the widespread premonitions, extraordinary and miraculous events took place. The chronicler Raoul Glabert described those that were witnessed in Orléans Cathedral: a marble statue of

Christ began weeping; one morning a monstrous wolf came in, took the bell rope between his teeth and rang matins; a fire destroyed half the city.

Wonders were reported from many different countries: rains of pebbles, blood and boundary stones; a whale emerged from the ocean, so large that his head was sighted early in the morning and his tail did not pass till three o'clock in the afternoon; ships were seen flying across the sky; Mount Vesuvius began spewing out lava and foul-smelling gas; a "horrible" comet appeared in the sky.

As the weeks and months went by, panic reached a fever pitch and everyone saw himself damned, condemned to everlasting torment.

And then the fateful date arrived.

Believers prostrated themselves in churches and waited for the stroke of doom. But nothing remarkable happened. Then, filled with love and gratitude toward the merciful God who had not annihilated the world, they shouted for joy, prayed fervently and began making pilgrimages. Those who had rashly given away their worldly goods may have gnashed their teeth a little, but their disappointment was outweighed by elation at their miraculous survival. On the whole, it was a beneficial operation: the poor had lost little and the rich had paid a tax on their unjust privileges.

Similarly, we may hope that at the beginning of the twenty-first century, when the anguish and terror have ended, mankind will feel relieved and start a reversal of social behavior.

THE CABIRI WILL RETURN
ON FLYING DRAGONS

According to Scandinavian mythology, at the end of the world the wolf Fenrir will devour the moon and blood will pour over the earth.

For the Mandaeans (also known as the Christians

of Saint John), four hundred and eighty thousand years will pass from the creation of the world till its end.

Such ancient beliefs have little substance, but more rational considerations support the view that the time is near when great planetary events will occur.

In 400 B.C. the most powerful weapon could cause the death of only one person; the explosive artillery shell could kill ten in the eighteenth century and twenty in 1914; a hundred thousand could be killed by the atomic bomb of 1945, two million by the hydrogen bomb of 1955; and in our time a four-hundred-megaton bomb can kill fifty million.

It is now possible for one man to wipe out all civilization on our planet. The stage is set for the annihilation that, according to traditional writings, will mark the beginning of a new cycle. And, considering the state of the world today, how can we believe that the supreme act of madness will not be committed?

There will again be a Deluge, survivors and a slow rebirth. Then, if we are to believe traditions, the Cabiri (Azazel, the Ases, Prometheus, the Nagas) will reappear on their flying dragons, which means that Instructors will come from another planet to teach the survivors who have fallen back into a primitive state.

THE UNCONSCIOUS AND DESTINY

We are now preparing for interplanetary travel in somewhat the same way as migratory birds prepare for crossing the Atlantic. We seem to know why we are making that effort, but the basic reasons lie in our genes and memory chromosomes.

Scientists seem to study nuclear fission, the design of spacecraft and the conditioning of astronauts because they want to advance science and conquer space, but it is probable that they are unconsciously working to perfect the instruments that will again loosen the polar icecaps and the Noah's Ark that will go to another planetary system with a group of pioneers and some selected samples of our destroyed civilization.

The end of the world will not occur until a few spacecraft reach their destination. But as soon as they do, it will mean the end of our earthly cycle. Everything will take place with perfect timing, as the apple ripens and rots before winter comes, and as pollen sets off on its journey before the cataclysm of cold.

Mathematicians might be able to calculate the period of ripening, the time when spacecraft will be sent out like pollen and the approximate date when Paris, New York, Moscow, Cairo, London, Rome, Tokyo and Hong Kong will be submerged in floods set off by ice floes from Greenland or the Antarctic. Such would be the mathematical destiny of our globe and our human race, of our cycle.

Modern man seems intent on hastening the end by developing nuclear weapons and spacecraft as rapidly as possible. But it would probably take only a little common sense, intelligence and love to prolong the cycle, because it will not end until everything is ready. Apocalyptic times do not simply arrive in accordance with a predetermined schedule; they are created by apocalyptic actions. In other words, worldwide cataclysms do not recur regularly, at fixed intervals. That belief belongs to false initiation.

CHAPTER 11

Ancient Views of
Cosmogony and World Endings

INITIATES PRECEDED PHYSICISTS by thousands of years
in their boldest theories on genesis and the space-time
continuum: *In the nonexistent, in the nothingness of
the ultrapast initial void, everything was procreated
with the existent of the ultrafuture universe.*

There was thus no creation of the world, no cosmogony, just as there is no time and there will be no
end.

I will use the word "cosmogony" not in its literal
meaning of "birth of the world," but in the meaning of
"explanation of life," or "explanation of what exists
and lives," setting aside all idea of birth and death,
beginning and end.

It is in this way that Hindu cosmogony must be
understood. A beginning and an end of the world are
only breaths of Brahma, frequencies of an energy that
is neither continuous nor alternating, but *electric*; that

is, it is propagated without determinate directions, by excitation, and is thus not a *current*.

THE COSMOGONY OF THE RIG-VEDA

The Hindu explanation of the universe is extremely subtle, since it leads to the conclusion that life is no more real than death, time or space. One can say that reality is as potential as potentiality is real.

We must therefore be cautious and thorough in analyzing the "creation" of the world according to the Rig-Veda:

There was neither being nor nonbeing, neither ether nor the canopy of the sky, neither enveloping nor enveloped... but only That One, He, breathing alone, alone with Her whose life he sustained in His bosom. Aside from Him, nothing existed which has since existed. The desire formed by His intelligence became the original seed [desire is energy]; the seed gradually became Providence, or sentient souls and matter or elements. She who is sustained by Him, in His bosom, was the lower part; and He, who observes, was the upper part. Who in this world knows exactly and can say from where and how that creation took place? The gods are later than that engendering of the world.

The idea of "creation" is foreign to Hindu theologians. For them, God did not *create* the universe: he *vomited* it. (Vomiting implies a creation from inner matter that belongs to the creator.) What they call creation is the birth of the elements, the elementary molecules, the senses and intelligence, a birth produced by Brahma by means of an uneven mixture of qualities: secondary emissions come from Purusha, the constructive principle.

In reality nothing takes place in this way, because everything is *maya* (illusion).

THE COSMOGONY OF MANU

Manu (in the Laws of Manu) explains the genesis of the universe in a seemingly different but actually identical way:

This world was plunged in imperceptible darkness and totally lacking in distinctive attributes; since it could be neither discovered by reasoning nor revealed, it seemed entirely given up to sleep. When *pralaya* [dissolution, chaos] came to an end, the Lord existing by himself, who is not within the scope of the external senses, appeared and unfolded nature. Having decided in his mind to make the various creatures emanate from his substance, he first produced the waters and placed a germ in them. This germ became an egg as shiny as gold, as bright as the heavenly body with a thousand rays, and in it the Supreme Being embodied himself in the form of Brahma, the ancestor of all beings.* After remaining in that egg a year of Brahma, the Lord separated it into two parts by his thought alone, and from those two parts he formed the sky and the earth; in the middle he placed the atmosphere, the eight celestial regions and the constant reserve of water.

Manu, also called Svayambhuva or Viraj, is "he whose power is immense." He is the first being of creation. Under the name of Viraj, he is the emanation of Brahma.

* This Hindu tradition of the Supreme Being transforming himself into an egg, taking a form, embodying himself to give birth to the universe, is common to all the cosmic beliefs of ancient peoples.

"Having divided his body into two parts, the Sovereign Master became half male and half female, and by uniting himself with his female part, he engendered Viraj."

The germ that fertilized the "golden womb" was called by the Hindus (as later by the Christians) the Spirit and the Word. The whole formed an initial trinity: Brahma or Nara the father, Nari the mother, Viraj the son. Later priests created the *trimurti*: Brahma the creator, Vishnu the preserver, Shiva the destroyer.

In the same way, and by the same phenomenon of deterioration, the Christians established the Holy Trinity: the Father, the Son and the Holy Spirit.

EXTRATERRESTRIAL ANCESTORS

"The sun made the division between day and night for men and the *devas*."

The *devas* are gods in the same way as the *asuras,* who later became demons, though without any great evil intention. The illustrious Varuna is an *asura*; Indra is a *deva*.

Varuna is a custodian of wisdom and a sovereign of justice. His symbol is the moon. With Mitra, he holds *maya,* which in this case does not mean "illusion," but "magic power." Indra, son of the sky and the earth, lives on Mount Meru, which stands at the center of the seven continents of the globe. According to mythologists, this mountain has a height of eighty-four thousand *yojanos* (one *yojano* equals about thirteen inches), but sixty thousand are underground. Perhaps it should be identified with the mysterious Agartha of esotericists. It is usually said to have a pyramidal shape (though it is also said to be conical, square or round) and its sides are of different colors: red on the north, white on the east, yellow on the south, black on the west.

"A month for mortals is a day and a night for the

pitris, deified human ancestors who live on other planets."

The beings that the Book of Manu calls *pitris* are thus extraterrestrials. Some of them came to Earth to act as the Initiators of human beings, who thanked them by deifying them.

THE AGES OF THE WORLD

In the Puranas Duty or Dharma is represented in the form of a bull whose four feet correspond to the four ages of the world:

—Krita: austerity, meditation; Golden Age.
—Treta: knowledge, sacrifice; Silver Age.
—Dvapara: worship; Bronze Age.
—Kali: praise, deterioration; Iron Age.

The Bhagavata Purana states that the world must perish by fire at the end of each age. There are four *pralayas,* or destructions of the world. They are named Naimittika, Prakritika, Nitya and Atyantika. They do not correspond to the four ages, as is often thought. According to the eminent Orientalist Eugène Burnouf, the matter is more complex:

Naimittika (accidental) destruction, whose cause is the sleep of Brahma, takes place at the end of each age; that is, after a thousand *caturyugas,* when the night of Brahma comes.

Prakritika (normal) destruction, that of the principles produced by nature, takes place at the expiration of the two periods of Brahma's life.

Then what are called "principles" in the Samkhya system, namely, intelligence, personality, the senses, the elements, etc.—all this returns to the bosom of nature.

Nitya (constant) destruction, which the Kaurma Purana places first, perhaps rightly, is that which occurs every day before our eyes. It is the perpetual succession of changes through which all beings pass or, as Vans Kennedy maintains, the extinction of life at night during sleep.

Atyantika (definitive) destruction is the identification of the individual soul with the supreme Brahma, an identification to which the yogi attains by his knowledge.

To sum up, as A. Roussel says in his *Cosmologie Hindoue,* mankind's salvation takes place by means of integration of the individual human personality into the divine personality.

Is this nirvana?

A SINGLE GOD IN ALL RELIGIONS

In genesis according to the Chaldeans, the union of Astart and El gave birth to the universe.

Babylonian genesis: Water is the primordial element, the sole god. All creation arises from the fusion between fresh water (Apsu) and salt water (Tiamat).

In ancient Elam the "Sovereign of the gods," builder of the universe, was the unique god, whose true name must not be revealed.

Phoenician mythology: The supreme god is El, but his true name is hidden from noninitiates. El appears to be the prototype of the creating god, borrowed by the Hebrews under the name of Elohim, the plural name of a single god.

For the ancient Persians, the supreme god was fire, Atar, father and son of Ahura Mazda, who became the creating god by identifying himself with his essence.

The cosmogony of the Persians gives twelve thousand years as the duration of our present universe. Ormazd, the uncreated creator and hypostasis of Ahura Mazda, first *thinks* the immaterial universe. He thus creates Ahriman (evil) who will struggle against him for nine thousand years. This will be the war of light against darkness, good against evil. After thinking the universe, Ormazd truly creates it, but we must understand that when his creative thought immaterially foresees the universe, it thereby gives it material consistence. This is the first known demonstration of parallel universes.

THE EVE OF THE CELTS

The Celts of Ireland worshiped the Great Goddess, Danu or Dana, who was called Epona or Arduina in Gaul. Celtic cosmogony attributes creation to the Mater or Great Goddess whose name is Eve or Aigue or Water (that is, source of life). The Celtic Eve does not represent the first woman taken from Adam's "rib."

The Hebrews, who created their mythology by borrowing from the Egyptians, Phoenicians, Celts, Hindus, etc., turned the El of the Phoenicians into Elohim, and the Eve of the Celts into Adam's wife. But the Celtic Eve is the Great Goddess; she is water, the source of all life, in which amino acids create the first elements of cellular life, the first proteins. In the rural dialects of southwestern and central France the word for water is still *ève*.

Jean Markale sensed this identity of water with the Celtic-Hebrew Eve when he wrote in his book *Les Celtes et la Civilisation Celtique,* "As for water, it is above all Fertility, creative Moistness, Mother Water; it is our Mother Eve, and the Deluge, far from being an expiatory catastrophe, is a return to the primordial Mother."

ANNUN, ABRED, GWENVED

In his preface to Kaledvoulc'h's book *Sous le Chêne des Druides* Philéas Lebesgue posits a Druidism strongly tinged with Christianity, but his cosmogony is interesting by the sole fact that it exists, since most historians of Celtic culture almost never pay any attention to the subject: "There are three circles of life, say the Triads. All life begins in Annun (the abyss, the dark depths) where the primordial fermentations begin, acquires knowledge through suffering in Abred (the world of necessity), and reaches fullness in the circle of whiteness, the sky or Gwenved."

The Barddas (Welsh book of theology) says that according to the Druids the physical world was constituted by four elements: *calas,* the origin of earth, stone and minerals; *gwyar,* the source of water; *fun,* air and gases; *uvel,* light, fire, heat.

The invisible world, or creative principle, is the *nwyvre* (serpent) from which all life flows. Life is made of *manred,* which is an immaterial wave, perhaps electricity, considering the etymology of the word: *man,* "nothing," and *red,* "running." *Manred* is also "the elements in their smallest division, in their ultimate atoms. Each atom is animated by the Supreme Being, who inhabits it entirely."

CHAPTER 12

☯☯

Initiation and the
Mysterious Unknown of Life

INITIATION IS A METHOD of general culture that is often misinterpreted. The word comes from the Latin *initium,* "beginning," and it must be understood that an initiate is *always a student,* even if he is called Master out of affectionate esteem. Physicists, astronomers and biologists are initiates in sciences unknown by laymen. Yet, rightly or wrongly, the word "initiation" has come to be associated almost exclusively with esotericism.

For adepts of occultism, the Initiate has become a mysterious, infallible person, almost invisible and untouchable, who possesses superhuman knowledge bequeathed to him by eminent Masters.

TABOO ON THE SECRETS OF ICA

One of my respected colleagues, a specialist in esotericism and fantastic science, has stated publicly (on

201

television) that he will not believe in Superior Ancestors until a twenty-thousand-year-old typewriter or motorcycle has been discovered.

It is an excellent philosophy but he carries it too far, even when he writes that he does not believe in flying saucers, extraterrestrials or Initiates who hold discussions in cafés.

"What is an Initiate?" he asks. "How can we recognize one?"

Those questions deserve an answer, and I will try to give one.

An Initiate is someone who has certain knowledge, often foreign to conventional science, and backs up its authenticity, usually by producing evidence.

Buddha, Pythagoras, Roger Bacon and Einstein were Initiates. So, presumably, are Dr. Cabrera, who knows the existence of Superior Ancestors, and the NASA scientists who look for antediluvian astronomical laboratories in Bolivia.

How were Dr. Cabrera and the American scientists "chosen" to know "things," secrets, caves? They "chose" themselves by earning that honor through their work, their faith and their faculties of apperception.

How do esoteric circles know of the existence of Initiates? Masters teach publicly, and it is up to esoteric circles to decide which of them bring light.

Moreover, esotericists and Initiates recognize and help each other. They also extend their help to all mankind. For example, Dr. Cabrera is an Initiate and I am not, yet he chose to reveal the genesis of our history to me, *and to give me the mission of making it public.*

But what about secrecy? Strictly speaking, there is no secrecy, there are only minds not sufficiently developed to understand and accept certain truths. Dr. Cabrera showed me some stones whose nature I must not divulge, because of the undesirable reactions that would be aroused in religious and political circles, as well as the general public. But he authorized me to reveal the "secrets" of Ica to anyone worthy. The Rosicrucians, for example, through the teachings of Raymond Bernard, their Grand Master in France, were the first to be informed of the revelations brought by the Ica stones.

Other eminent figures in esotericism were also informed, and thus, between 1972 and 1974, there was continuation of a chain of transmission whose first link was forged at the dawn of man's existence.

THE SIN OF SEEKING THE SELF

In empirical initiation pseudosages are still at the stage of seeking the supreme self and traditional illumination. Far be it from me to deny the real initiation and teaching that can be drawn from meditation; too many genuine sages have proved its effectiveness and virtue. But it must be recognized that, particularly in India, multitudes of ignorant adepts have wasted their lives on sterile psychic exercises.

In the same way, aspiration to beatitude has become a disease. For those afflicted with it, the supreme mission is the quest for the self. Hence the constant refrain of false sages and initiates: seeking their unknown, eternal and divine self. They do not doubt for one moment that the gods are reflected in their states of mind, thoughts and intuitions, and even in their sweat and buttocks.

It is true, but in the same way as a mirror reflects the image of a face even if it is hideous, and in some cases reflects a hideous image even when the face is beautiful. Two factors are involved: the mirror may distort what it reflects, and the face may be distorted, deteriorated, ravaged.

It is obvious that when the self has undergone deep, irreversible deterioration it will act as a distorting mirror, giving a false, ludicrous image of divinity and the essence of all things. And yet how many megalomaniac spiritualists undertake the quest for the Grail in their own personalities! They concentrate, turn inward, study themselves minutely, sometimes with disapproval but usually with admiration, and finally drift into madness.

As if the true goal of life were to discover God, to lift all the veils that cover the Holy of Holies! Imagine unscrupulous politicians, businessmen and pimps finding their selves in their nauseous inner depths! Imagine trees, mountains, clouds, angels and God himself seeking their selves!

Universal order and laws are not decreed for an infinite number of selves, most of which must disappear prematurely, but for the great self of the Whole, for the totality that can radiate its harmony in the body only if the legs, arms, neck and back are closely united, commune and participate in a single soul. If the left leg tries to dance a jig and the right one a tango, the dancer will fall on his face.

The universe is an organism, a dancer that must be perfectly harmonious.

SUPERSTITIONS OF SAGES AND BIOLOGISTS

Our concept of the infinite does not allow us to understand how everything is in everything; otherwise the quest for the self, even with a distorted mirror, would lead to the discovery of God. And it would be a foolish procedure, since the image of perfection is everywhere: in a rose, in a bird's feather, in the texture of a grain of sand. Why look for it in the least original and authentic part of nature: man?

If everything is in everything, what is above is like what is below. This axiom, one of the keys to initiation, has always been contested by scientists, even the most eminent.

INITIATION AND THE MYSTERIOUS UNKNOWN

One of the most patent proofs of the authenticity of initiation and the transmission of nonveiled, nonsecret knowledge lies precisely in the belief that a grain of sand, a bicycle pump, a stalk of wheat, a beetle and Niels Bohr have basically the same constituents, the same kind of soul, sensitivity and intelligence.

Most scientists still deny that essential identity that implies, for example, that a carpenter's plane can have a certain level of happiness, feelings of hatred or love, an intelligence and an understanding of its environment and itself.

Yet a hard blow has recently been struck against scientists' superstitions, not by a luminary of the scientific world, but by an American polygraph expert named Cleve Backster.

FEELINGS IN PLANTS

A polygraph, or lie detector, measures changes in certain physiological functions associated with anger, lying, pity, etc. When a feeling appears or changes intensity, this fact is recorded in the lines traced by the machine.

One day Cleve Backster wondered if he could detect feeling in a plant. He attached polygraph electrodes to a leaf of a house plant and decided to see if he could cause a pain reaction by burning the leaf with the flame of a match. As soon as this thought came into his mind, without his having actually struck a match, the polygraph recorded a violent reaction.

Other investigators were soon studying the "Backster effect" on various kinds of plants. They reported plant reactions to threats, pain and fear.

Tests showed that a plant feels fear at the approach of an animal that intends to eat it. When they are threatened by danger, some plants go into a kind of coma to escape suffering. They show joy in the presence of someone who loves them, and terror when someone wishes them harm.

One of Backster's experiments was particularly striking. Six men drew lots to see which of them would destroy one of two plants that Backster had placed in a room. Backster himself did not know who the "murderer" would be. When the victim had been destroyed, he connected the surviving plant to a polygraph and had each of the six men come back into the room. As soon as the guilty one appeared, the polygraph needle showed intense emotion in the plant.

It seems that a plant's power of apperception is manifested whenever harm is done to any form of organic life: shellfish, eggs, human tissue, hair, etc. From this it has been inferred that everything that exists is alive and has a kind of consciousness infused throughout its elements. There is thus nothing truly inanimate in the universe. A grain of sand, a lump of metal, a hill and a biologist's brain are all alive, and all belong to the same primordial, ultimate organism.

This discovery of twentieth-century science is a clear demonstration of initiatory knowledge, because what Backster learned in 1966 had been known by Initiates for more than four thousand years.

We may assume that in the near future scientists will also acknowledge other phenomena that are still called occult or supranormal: the memory of things and places, ghosts, clairvoyance, telluric currents, sorcery and other manifestations of the Mysterious Unknown.

MAGIC CURES

The consciousness and intelligence that seem to exist in all realms of matter, and the plant-human interaction whose effects we are beginning to verify, give meaning to certain apparently obscure theories of ancient metaphysics.

Thus it is now possible to accept the idea that continents and oceans can determine their own evolution to some extent, and perhaps set off cataclysms against oppressive human societies.

In a fascinating little book (*Brion-Gençay: Mystères de leur Histoire*), Jacques Pineau evokes the emotional and somewhat magic bonds between plants and human beings.

He cites the experiment of Dr. Jean Barry of Bordeaux, who appreciably slowed the growth of parasitic mushrooms cultivated in Petri dishes by having his assistants concentrate their will on them. The experiment was conducted in nine sessions, with thirty-one dishes of mushrooms. The ten assistants stood five feet away from them and concentrated on them for fifteen minutes each time. The mushrooms in thirty-one of the thirty-nine dishes had their development significantly retarded.

The strong will of a gifted person can act on a plant, writes Pineau. Emanations of human love are known to have a beneficial effect on plants, but the process can also work in the opposite direction, as has been demonstrated in sorcery for thousands of years.

Pineau's family once had a gardener named Rousseau who was a genuine sorcerer. He writes about him as follows:

His way of treating sick people was always the same, no matter what their illness. He asked for a lock of the patient's hair, took it into the forest, chose a healthy young tree, cut it with a pruning knife, put the hair into the incision and tied it with raffia. He then walked around the tree, chanting incantations in a harsh language that was not Latin and came from the depths of time. The tree immediately began wasting away and the patient began recovering, as we were able to see for ourselves. The tree he chose was, preferably, a young ash. To hasten recovery, he made a little cross from twigs of the ash and put it under the patient's pillow.

Thanks to the experiments of Backster and Dr. Barry, it is now possible to explain that magic which, until recently, belonged to the realm of superstition.

We can even replace Rousseau's unknown incantations with equally effective words that appeal to the tree's benevolent feelings: "Ash tree, my friend, give your sap and your life in a sublime sacrifice to save So-and-So."

It seems that such magic—which is actually unjust, since the strong is sacrificed to the weak, the healthy to the sick—has long been known by empirics. It involves a transfer (in the occult sense of the word) of life potential with the consent and voluntary sacrifice of a plant.

But by what sublime altruistic sentiment do plants consent to their own destruction?

It is likely that scientists exaggerate in their conclusions on the intelligence and emotional faculties of plants, for otherwise it would be possible for an herb to change its effects at will; mint, for example, could become a soporific, a laxative or even a violent poison. Yet Cleve Backster has undeniably made important contributions that form a bridge between conventional science and empirical knowledge.

An immense field of investigation is now opening up if, as is already suspected in theoretical physics, minerals are really endowed with intelligence and emotional reactions. We can glimpse the secrets behind the sorcerer's power to conjure, cast spells and cure; the alchemist's relentless efforts to reconcile the supranormal privileges of sulfur, mercury, vitriol, water and fire; the Mysterious Unknown of perfumes, saps, philters and the magic effects of a touch. All this results from an emotional harmony among human beings, plants and minerals, and from the invisible forces that surround, observe and condition us.

SPIRIT TABLES

Open-mindedness toward everything that lies beyond our present knowledge should not lead us into gullibility and blind faith. Theoretically, nothing is impossible in the universe, but there is reason to be wary of certain manifestations called supranormal.

It seems that there is a great deal of vagueness and credulity in a common kind of spiritualistic experiment performed with the aid of a table. It takes place as follows: the table must be three-legged and light, and therefore easy to maneuver; several people sit around it and form a circle of hands, touching each other's little fingers; the participants concentrate and, aloud, ask a spirit to manifest himself; if contact is successfully made, the spirit answers questions by tapping out answers in code: one tap for A, two for B, three for C, and so on.

There is usually a leader who is rightly or wrongly believed to be a medium. In most cases, it is he or she who asks the questions, but any participant may ask one. With very rare exceptions, however, the table always tilts in the direction of the leader, either directly toward him or a little to his left or right, depending on the position of the table legs.

If there is no real leader, it is unlikely that the spirit will manifest himself, i.e., that the table will move— unless one of the participants intensely desires it.

It is customary to ask the spirit his name and if he knows someone present or is someone's guide. He usually answers that he is the guide of one of the participants, who of course feels highly honored, and he often says that he knew such-and-such a relative, who, being dead, cannot contradict him.

Conversation then takes place on a drearily commonplace level: X will soon receive a letter, Y will learn of a marriage or a death, Z will find a soul mate by the end of the year.

Or you may be warned of a danger. What kind of danger? When? The spirit doesn't like to be specific. You'll face a danger in the near future, that's all, and if you go on annoying him, he won't answer any more questions.

"You mustn't try to push him when he's already been nice enough to give you a warning," someone will be sure to say.

And if nothing happens, no one will accuse the spirit of having lied; instead, he will be thanked for having warded off the peril.

If the leader is a cultivated person, the spirit may express a few intelligent ideas, but if the leader is ignorant, the answers are nearly always on a rather low intellectual level. Try asking a table-tapping spirit how to say "truth" in Sanskrit, ancient Persian and Greek!

Nevertheless I believe it is possible for an answer to go beyond the level of conscious knowledge. In that case it may borrow from a superior knowledge that lies in our unconscious. In short, the explanation of "table tapping" may be related to a phenomenon of exteriorization of the unconscious.

THE UNKNOWN SELF THAT WE OPPRESS

The human brain is a vast electrical complex whose active portion is said to be composed of about two billion neurons. It has large reserves whose function is not known, and which do not seem to be used: the seven to eight billion neurons that compose the cellular elements of the nervous system.

The properties of neurons are related to conduction

of nerve impulses and excitations. Neurons gather and transmit information in the manner of a computer. They give responses to stimuli and are the basis of the organization of cerebral work. They are thought to control the individual's conduct and intracerebral language or communication.

For the neurobiologist, the brain is still a vast world whose basic nature is nearly unknown, but some investigators believe that the eight billion apparently unused neurons may play a fundamental part in what is called the Mysterious Unknown of the self.

On this hypothesis, the unused portions of the brain and the spinal cord are related to a second personality containing a fund of knowledge and a will to action that function unknown to the consciousness manifested by the first personality. This almost totally unexplored universe constitutes the unconscious, which serves as a storage area for knowledge, acts, motivations and behavior not gathered and recorded in the conscious mind.

In certain circumstances, particularly when the conscious mind relaxes its vigilance and authoritarian control, the unconscious feels a strong need to throw off its constraints and manifest itself. It lacks means of biological transmission, since most of the appropriate usable channels are controlled by the conscious mind, but it has such fantastic powers of concentration that its capacity for storing knowledge is theoretically unlimited.

If we could draw on that immense library of information, we would be immeasurably more intelligent and have almost total knowledge of everything. Such knowledge may be transmitted in neurons or unknown parts of the brain by heredity. All knowledge given to the human race since its beginning may be stored there, with the risks of deterioration involved in transmission: degradation of energy, adulteration, effacement, etc.

Aside from his work, the Initiate derives his superiority from the fact that he is able to draw on more than his two billion active neurons. What he acquires in this way is usually manifested through the ordinary means of expression.

REBELLION IN ZONE 2

The empiric who succeeds in freeing certain powers of his unconscious acts without the permission of the conscious mind, in what might be called an "illegal" way, and the knowledge that thus filters through is tainted by error and incompleteness.

To understand the mechanism of "table tapping," we must distinguish three zones within each individual:

Zone 1: the conscious or first personality.

Zone 2: the unconscious or second personality, between consciousness and the unknown self.

Zone 3: the unknown self.

The first personality (zone 1) controls our usual life. The second personality (zone 2) contains complexes, desires, obsessions, aspirations, repressions, etc. The unknown self (zone 3) records hereditary knowledge and knowledge that touches consciousness lightly without being able to penetrate it. It does this easily because it has billions of unused neurons at its disposal.

The second personality does not have this privilege, however, and because of its position between zones 1 and 3, it feels hemmed in and persecuted, for it has neither the conscious mind's powers of expression nor the unknown self's powers of absorption and choice. It has the impression that it *could* be called on to control visible human behavior but, by a great injustice, is never given a chance to do so.

Zone 2 is thus the dwelling place of another self—reticent, confused, sometimes ashamed—which becomes rebellious because it feels oppressed. Hence its desire to make itself known and express itself as soon as it has the opportunity.

That opportunity arises when the conscious mind relaxes its vigilance and no longer keeps close watch on the circuits of information: during dreams, in certain forms of meditation and, at a lower level, in clairvoyance and "table tapping."

During dreams the subconscious is totally liberated, which allows peaceful coexistence between the unconscious and the conscious mind; a person who never dreamed would become a prey to his zone 2 and would be in an almost constant state of delirium.

The subconscious is also liberated by meditation in the Hindu system, which consists in emptying the mind, and by clairvoyance when the subject is in a state of complete receptivity.

As an artificial system, "table tapping" is a means of bringing out information that the conscious mind usually condemns or represses. When the chain of hands is formed around the table, a center of energy accumulation seems to be created by the participants. One of them, the medium (or several persons), receives this energy and uses it to cause the physical phenomenon of semilevitation.

The participants must not oppose any resistance to the experiment; they must empty their minds and be receptive to any intervention from a pseudo-Beyond. If one of them leaves his surveillance centers in a state of alert, he may break the spell (the chain of energy concentration). The medium will then say that someone undesirable is present and must leave.

Many such experiments are falsified by dishonesty on the part of the medium, but my study involves only experiments without deliberate trickery. The participants are in good faith; they will not consciously cheat, but they will do so unconsciously.

The goal is to allow the unconscious of the medium (or several people) to manifest itself. When that condition has been met, the medium's second personality can use temporarily unguarded channels of communication and externalize itself by tapping out messages, thus trespassing in an area normally forbidden to it: thoughts, acts and spoken language. It uses these things with the full complicity of the participants' first personalities.

As a preliminary, the medium asks the usual question: "Spirit, are you here? Tap once if you are."

The unconscious suggests the answer and there is an automatic increase in the pressure of the hands, barely perceptible but enough to make the table tilt and tap once.

It is likely that, in addition to the physical pressure, there is also a force of magnetic attraction and repulsion caused by an electrical phenomenon. If so, a negative pole in the table may be repelled by a positive pole formed in the medium's hands. The force then becomes powerful enough to tilt the unstable three-legged table.

Watching an experiment, one sees the participants concentrate when the table tilts, and then relax so that it can regain its balance. At this stage the medium's electric potential is redistributed through the whole chain of hands.

The honest medium does not cheat, strictly speaking, but he helps his second personality to express itself. The lower world of the unconscious lacks the normal means of expressing itself correctly but, in complicity with the dormant conscious minds of the participants, it can carry on a commonplace conversation conditioned by their lower desire-thoughts.

"Spirit, what is your name?"

The unconscious is intelligent enough to spell out a name, and shrewd enough to choose the name of someone known to at least one of the people present.

Then come questions suggested or even imposed by desire-thoughts: marriages, accidents, encounters, letters, journeys. They are nearly always of a kind that can be answered simply: yes, no, soon, maybe. No dates, places, names or specific circumstances can be obtained, because the unconscious does not know them.

These games are basically inconsequential, but afterward a certain value is attributed to them by the awakened conscious minds of the participants.

When contact is made with the second personality, the answers are elementary and disappointing. But if contact could be made with the superior unknown self, or third personality, sensational revelations would result: the table might describe a cure for cancer, and would probably have the power to announce the future.

Unfortunately, however, "spirits" have never given information useful to mankind. It is as if the Beyond had no desire to help the living. But perhaps the same could be said of "Initiates."

CHAPTER 13

Strange Things
Between Heaven and Earth

THE EXISTENCE OF FLYING SAUCERS, much less of extraterrestrials living on our planet, has not been proved. Scientists are interested in the matter, accept the phenomenon of UFOs, but refuse to venture very far into the realm of speculation.

Professor Louis Leprince-Ringuet, whose honesty and impartiality I admire, says that "a scientist should always be open to any observations that may occur, so we do not reject the possibility of anything, even of flying saucers. One of the most valuable arguments would be discovery of an object or a piece of matter abandoned by space people. But we have nothing of the sort."

This lack of evidence is regrettable, and so is the tendency of many Ufologists to mistake their desires for realities.

Some of them have gone so far as to claim that

"fairy circles" in meadows are caused by landings of extraterrestrials, when their real explanation is well known: they come from an underground cryptogamic network that is responsible for nearby sterile areas.

In October 1972 a small tornado ravaged a wooded hillside at Collet Redon, near Montaroux, France. That kind of miniature disaster is common in many parts of France, where everyone has seen trees that have been twisted and uprooted by tornadoes. In the past such happenings were classified as whims of nature; in our time they are regarded as interplanetary incidents!

Even the usually serious *Bulletin du G.E.P.A.*, a quarterly magazine devoted to study of aerial phenomena, published a long illustrated article on the Collet Redon tornado; it seems that some remarkably stupid extraterrestrials tried to land their spacecraft on a steep hillside bristling with trees and walls. Why? The article neglects to tell us.

A RECEPTION CENTER
FOR EXTRATERRESTRIALS

Claude Vorilhon of Clermont-Ferrand, France, feels it is disgraceful to make our extraterrestrial visitors land under such unfavorable conditions. We ought to build a spaceport for them and, while we are at it, a comfortable residence to house them. They expect that courteous treatment. How does Claude Vorilhon know? They told him so.

The story goes back to December 13, 1973, when Vorilhon felt himself "called" to the Puy de la Vache, an extinct volcano ten miles southwest of Clermont-Ferrand. There he found an extraterrestrial waiting for him. The visitor was only about four feet tall. He had a black beard, and of course he wore green plastic tights. He spoke flawless French and his flying saucer, of the standard type, was red, white and blue, like the French flag.

"Claude Vorilhon," he said, in substance, "I've chosen you because you came into the world in 1945, the year of the first atomic bomb on Earth, and because you were born of a Jewish father and a Christian mother. I'm going to give you some instructions, but since I forgot to bring any writing materials with me from my home planet, come back tomorrow with pencil and paper. And don't tell anyone you've seen me."

The next day he gave Vorilhon some secrets that, naturally, were not to be divulged to anyone, but he allowed him to reveal that his home planet was only one light-year away and that his flying saucer had a cruising speed of thirteen million miles per second. His main public revelation concerned our origin: we are descended from synthetic living beings who were deported to Earth long ago. The extraterrestrials regard us as their children to some extent, and they want to help us behave more sensibly.

In conclusion, he suggested that we show our appreciation to the space people by building them a residence worthy of their knowledge and the benefits they will bestow on us at a future date. They prefer to have it built in a place with a mild climate, such as Monte Carlo, Tahiti, Miami or Hollywood.

This prompted Claude Vorilhon to found an organization called the Movement for Welcoming the Extraterrestrials Who Created Mankind.

It is noteworthy that in spite of their formidable scientific knowledge, the little green men of our mother planet cannot put up the funds needed to build their residence here. They are counting on the generosity of their earthly children.

FLYING TRAINS AND
A MARTIAN PILOT IN 1897

It would be pointless to dwell on the thousands of reports from apparently trustworthy people—mediums, lawyers, policemen—who have seen flying saucers and Martians when radars near the landing sites registered no images of celestial objects. It is as if—and why not? —flying saucers had no material consistency and could be perceived only by the human organism. Uncorroborated sightings cannot be given much credence, but they at least deserve to be recorded, for whatever they may be worth.

According to extremely doubtful reports from Argentina, there are underwater flying saucer bases in the Gulfs of San Tatias and San Jorge, off the coast of Patagonia.

In that same country UFOs have taken the form of "trains." A businessman named Francisco Zamor, and five other people, had to stop their car on the road from Difunta Correa to San Juan and wait for the crossing of a railway carriage about a hundred feet long, with all its windows lighted. But there are no tracks in that place.

At Santiago del Estero, still in Argentina, the mysterious "train," this time about a hundred and fifty feet long, came down in a forest, then flew away in the form of a fireball.

At the same place the same "train" (or one like it) was later seen by other witnesses.

In my opinion, such stories do not encourage rational minds to accept the wild statements made by too many Ufologists.

The enigma of Aurora, Texas, seems more worthy of attention. According to detailed reports, a flying machine crashed there in April 1897. At that time, of course, it could not have been an earthly airplane. The body of the pilot was buried without examination. An American UFO organization would like to exhume it to see if the pilot was from Earth or some other planet. For years there was a rumor in Aurora that a Martian was buried in the local cemetery.

CAPTAIN LEMOS FERREIRA'S REPORT

Alvaro Curado e Melo, my friend and correspondent in Lisbon, has sent me an account that is particularly interesting because the events involved were given very serious attention by the Portuguese government. They were kept secret for two months, then made public by the journalist Saraiva Mendes and published by the *Diaro Illustrado* on November 16, 1957.

On September 4, 1957, a group of F-84 aircraft took off from Ota at 8:21 P.M. They were under the command of Captain Lemos Ferreira; the three other pilots were Manuel Carlos Neves Marcelino, Alberto Augusto Perreira Gomes Covas and Salvador Alberto Oliveira. They intended to make a routine night flight on a triangular course marked by Ota-Grenade, Portalegre and Coruche. They reached an altitude of twenty-five thousand feet over Redondo. It was a clear, cloudless night with an oblique visibility of fifty miles. Grenade appeared directly below at 9:06.

"We were about to make a sixty-degree turn to head for Portalegre," said Captain Lemos Ferreira, "when I saw a luminous, spherical object just above the horizon. Surprised, I continued on my course, without turning, so that I could observe the object, and I reported it to my companions by radio. Marcelino told me that he also saw it. What struck us most about it was its flickering and the way its central core constantly changed color: it went from dark green to orangish yellow to bright red.

"It seemed to be stationary . . . but we could not come any closer to it, as if it wanted to maintain the distance between us and it. It remained the same till we reached Portalegre, but as we approached Coruche it gave us the impression of being much nearer and losing altitude.

"We were flying between Sousel and Fronteira when a small circle came from the object. It was also luminous, but did not flicker. It moved upward. Then we saw another circle, at a lower altitude, followed a minute later by two others with a reddish color. They were apparently quite near, a few thousand feet below us.

"I had just decided that we could not approach them when the luminous object, which had meanwhile taken on an oval shape, abruptly dived and then rapidly climbed toward us. The four circles did the same. They all passed behind us and slightly above us.

"My pilots were thrown into great confusion and broke formation. We returned to Ota without further incident and landed at 10:05."

The luminous object had been seen from the airfield, and conversation among the pilots had been heard on a frequency of 118.5 megacycles.

MARTIANS WITH SILICONE SHELLS

I regard the story reported by Alvaro Curado e Melo as perfectly admissible and authentic. It is such honest, verifiable reports that advance the study of UFOs.

But unfortunately there are visionaries, impostors and gullible people who distort the situation and make it appear ridiculous. There are also practical jokers who amuse themselves by telling preposterous stories.

"The inhabitants of the star Epsilon have sent a message to Earth," one of my colleagues, a journalist who specializes in "mysterious news," announced in 1973.

In my opinion, the star Epsilon is remarkable mainly by its absence from the known sky. In other words, it was invented out of whole cloth.

Here is the message said to have been sent by the Epsilonians: "We live on the planet that you call Epsilon, which is the sixth in a system of seven. Our planet has a moon, and we have just sent out a space probe, which is now in the orbit of your moon."

The same journalist, who always cites the names of real or invented scientists in support of his stories, maintains that a famous astrophysicist believes that Mars is inhabited by creatures with thick silicone shells that are impervious to cosmic rays. They are able to go into suspended animation for thousands of years and make water flow from stones.

In view of such stories—flying trains, messages from Epsilonians, Martians with silicone shells—it is easy to understand why scientists are reluctant to take UFOs seriously. Yet the problem exists. The number of inhabited planets in the universe may be almost infinite, and they must be inhabited by beings essentially like us, beings who think and speculate as we do, and dream of making contact across interstellar space.

THE PLURALITY OF INHABITED WORLDS

In all times it has been known that other worlds are inhabited, that the earth is round and that it moves through the sky in harmony with the stars.

Anaximander, Origen and Descartes taught that universes were dynamic, that they were cyclically destroyed and reproduced by a combination of the same elements.

"Even in ancient times," wrote Sylvain Bailly, "the idea of the plurality of worlds was adopted by philosophers who had enough genius to realize how great it is, and how worthy it is of the Author of Nature."

"Anaxagoras taught the inhabitability of the moon as an article of philosophical belief," Camille Flammarion wrote in his book *La Pluralité des Mondes Habités* (1877). "He maintained that, like our globe, the moon had bodies of water, mountains and valleys. He was a famous advocate of the idea of the earth's motion. It should be noted that his opinion turned envious fanatics against him, and that for having stated that the sun is larger than the Peloponnesus he was persecuted and nearly put to death."

Anaxagoras was mistaken about the inhabitability of the moon, but it was an extraordinary idea for his time, and it shows his genius.

Pythagoras taught universal gravitation and the plurality of worlds. Lucretius shared his opinion: "In other regions of space there are beings, mortals and worlds."

THE TOWER OF BABEL:
A LAUNCHING SITE

The myth of the Tower of Babel has perhaps not been studied from the proper viewpoint. Here is how the Bible presents it, in Genesis 11:1–9:

> Once upon a time all the world spoke a single language and used the same words. As men journeyed in the east, they came upon a plain in the land of Shinar and settled there. They said to one another, "Come, let us make bricks and bake them hard"; they used bricks for stone and bitumen for mortar. "Come," they said, "let us build ourselves a city and a tower with its top in the heavens, and make a name for ourselves; or we shall be dispersed all over the earth." Then the Lord came down to see the city and tower which mortal men had built, and he said, "Here they are, one people with a single language, and now they have started to do this; henceforward nothing they have a mind to do will be beyond their reach. Come, let us go down there and confuse their speech, so that they will not understand what they say to one another."

So the Lord dispersed them from there all over the earth, and they left off building the city. That is why it is called Babel, because the Lord there made a babble of the language of all the world; from that place the Lord scattered men all over the face of the earth.

The story is unclear and its explanation is unsatisfactory. After the Deluge, men decided to build a city with a great tower. Their stated purpose was to "make a name for themselves." I see nothing sacrilegious in that, since all civilizations have had the ambition of immortalizing their acquired knowledge by building structures that are consecrated to the glory of the Lord, either directly or through his privileged creation: man. But God did not see it that way, and he was also displeased by the fact that men all spoke the same language, so he decided to disperse them and "confuse their speech."

Was that decision divine or diabolical? Or is the summary explanation given in the Bible an invention by a scribe who tried to add a little coherence to the story?

On the assumption that the story has a certain basis in truth, another explanation can be attempted, using data from Chaldean mythology.

Xisuthros was the king who ruled Chaldea after the Deluge. He and his three sons were the first gods who shared the postdiluvian world. From them were descended a race of giants who conceived the impious idea of building a tower. God unleashed a storm against them and dispersed them, and someone whose identity is not revealed cast "unknown words" among men.

Greek mythology speaks of the Titans, civilizing heroes to whom the invention of the arts and magic is attributed. They were surely not of earthly origin, and resembled the erudite extraterrestrial "angels" of the *Book of Enoch*. They decided to pile mountains on top of each other to scale Olympus; that is, to defy God.

Here again we find the myth of the Tower of Babel. The idea of building a structure that would reach into the heavens may mean that the Titans wanted to return to their home.

Within the framework of this adventurous hypothesis we may imagine that at a time when the human race was relearning to till the soil and speak, the Titans knew how to build a rocket launching site. Their attempt failed and they remained on Earth, but from them earthlings absorbed foreign words and speech patterns that were the origin of different languages.

This idea is not implausible if we consider that traditions all over the world speak of angels or initiators who came from the stars before the Deluge and immediately after it. Furthermore it bears a logical relation to known facts: the mysterious *pistas* of Nasca, if they are antediluvian; the Ica stones, which are undoubtedly antediluvian; and the civilization of the prehistoric astronomers who made drawings representing the appearance of the Gum nebula forty thousand years ago.

CHAPTER 14

☜☞

UFOs: Serious Business

ALTHOUGH Professor Pierre Guérin of the Paris Astrophysical Institute is a declared adversary of writers in the field of "parallel science," he accepts the possibility of extraterrestrials living in planetary systems other than ours.

He conjectures that the mental processes of intelligent species in other parts of the universe must be quite different from ours, and that their mode of expression might not be perceived by earthly human beings. In that case their knowledge could not be communicated to us, especially since it would be the product of a scientific civilization much older than ours.

If extraterrestrials succeed in sending us messages, says Pierre Guérin, it is unlikely that we will be able to decipher them, since extraterrestrial technology is based on physical concepts that are alien and inaccessible to us.

This opinion does not stand up under scientific or common-sense analysis. If extraterrestrials are far more scientifically advanced than we are, for that very reason they are obviously intelligent enough to communicate with us on our level if they want to.

Contrary to the theories of prehistorians, I believe that man's alleged descent from the ape is not the most logical hypothesis, and in any case it seems impossible that our species was born on Earth. I therefore maintain that our genesis goes back countless billions of centuries if we belong to an extraterrestrial animal lineage, and only a few million years if we are an exceptional case, a privilege, in the realm of earthly living creatures.

But if man is a privileged exception, we must envision his appearance not only on a distant planet in the remote past, before a migration to our solar system, but also on our relatively young planet, at a much more recent time.

Unfortunately this mystery will probably never be elucidated; to advance on this path of knowledge, we have no choice but to replace faltering experimental science with the admittedly uncertain light of intellectual speculation.

THE COMING RACE

On the hypothesis of multiple inhabited worlds, we must assume the existence of civilizations much more advanced than ours. That is what Pierre Guérin tells us, and he is not worried by the possibility that our world may soon end, or that our species may undergo a fantastic mutation. But those who are called Initiates believe that the end of our earthly cycle is very near and that the survivors will undergo a process of biological evolution bordering on mutation.

The problem of relations between earthlings and

extraterrestrials will then cease, because there will no longer be an earthly human race. Instead, there will be a new race, one that is already being referred to beforehand as the Mutants.

We thus return to the idea of Guérin's intelligent extraterrestrial species, endowed with superthought and a psychic makeup different from ours—but, of course, beings that belong to such species are not human.

WHAT DOES A VIRUS SAY?

Despite their supposedly different nature, we must consider the possibility that visitors from space may react to us as we react to viruses, microbes, neutrinos, an aurora borealis, an intuition or an idea; that is, with the simplistic, falsely rational attitude that an astronomer takes toward a star, a biologist toward a cell, an average man toward a speck of dust, a poet toward the words that express his thoughts.

We believe that we psychically and intellectually inhabit our bodies, from the brain to the soles of the feet, but nothing is less certain. We have no precise knowledge of our mental processes, or of "inspiration," apperception and intuition, which may well be phenomena external to our integral selves, and perhaps to our galactic universe.

It is not impossible that most or even all of our ideas belong to an alien center, as a photon belongs to the sun.* If so, there is scarcely any possibility of direct communication between our ideas and "us," except in the manner of occultists, that is, by an operation similar to the process employed by a medium, one that helps us imagine the inner nature of reality.

---

* In any case our ideas and our selves belong only relatively to our space-time universe. Our mental and psychic processes are not born at the moment when we come into the world: they go back millions of years earlier. Ultimately, everything flows from and remains in interaction with all the elements of the universe, with all space-times.

Primohistory, which I wish to substitute for obsolete prehistory, is being strengthened through the years by discoveries made all over the world. At the same time, ideas that do not fit into the cramped categories of conventional thinkers, but are on the scale of the universes lying at the edge of our awareness, are beginning to be accepted by the increasingly numerous scientists traveling the path toward enlightenment under the impetus of imagination, the subconscious and the intelligence of memory chromosomes.

It is likely that there will soon be contacts between extraterrestrials and earthlings. We may also assume that such contacts are already taking place and that they even govern our individual and collective lives, but that we are unaware of them, not because of technological inadequacy but perhaps because, like those attributed to God, the designs of extraterrestrials must not yet be known.

SANTA CLAUS OR WEREWOLF OF THE COSMOS?

I do not claim that the coming of extraterrestrials would necessarily be harmful to our civilization, but elementary caution requires us to give at least brief consideration to various situations that might be created by such an event.

Millions of Ufologists tend to attribute extremely benevolent feelings to our future visitors, and it is hard to tell whether that attitude stems from naïveté, idealism or fear.

According to the Bible, the angels brought us knowledge previously unknown to us: metal smelting, making of weapons, shields, cosmetics, etc. But the symbol of those Instructors was Lucifer, and their knowledge led to the worldwide Deluge.

It seems that in the remote past the civilizations of

the Near East and America benefited from favorable attention by extraterrestrials, perhaps because those visitors were not in a position to act as colonizers. It is generally assumed that they were only a small group of survivors from a doomed planet, and that they therefore came to Earth as castaways.

But what would happen if extraterrestrials came as conquerors, equipped with a technology far superior to ours and assured of help from their home planet?

We expect help from the sky, and yet, when they are studied in depth, most of the conjectures we make on that subject ought to give us more fear than hope.

We believe that since extraterrestrials are theoretically more intelligent than we are, they are wise, kind and obliging. As if the earthly geniuses who invented gunpowder, war planes and atomic bombs were saints! As if the whole history of civilization did not show that human beings have always tried to settle their political, economic and religious differences by the use of force!

We have good reason to believe that after the euphoria of the first few moments, contact with extraterrestrials would be followed by a conflict with incalculable consequences.

SUPERBRAINS IN EARTHLY BODIES

Futurologists are unanimous in saying that the acceleration of knowledge is causing tension between the intellect, which is going too fast, and the physical body, which cannot keep up. Man thus seems condemned to become a superbrain inhabiting a degenerate body. He may even become a stagnant, vegetating physical creature sheltering an all-powerful brain that produces movement and all other effort by the sole force of its will.

Without going to that extreme, we can entertain the

possibility that our visitors will be physically inferior to us, and perhaps shorter-lived. In that case, if their science enables them to transplant their brains into our bodies, they will probably do so—without hatred or malevolence, with only the indifference we feel toward the rose we pluck or the apple we eat. For it is as logical to assume that we were created to sustain the Superior Visitors as that the apple was created for us to eat and the rose for us to admire.

THEY WILL CARRY DEATH ON THEM

If interplanetary contacts take place, circumstances impossible for us to imagine now will undoubtedly arise and, even with goodwill on both sides, some of them may set off a conflict that will result in annihilation of the whole earthly population.

There is no shortage of reasons for concern! For example, the Visitors may have an urgent need to settle in large numbers on our planet, which is already insanely overpopulated.

They may be decimated by earthly diseases to which their bodies have not developed immunity, but it is even more likely that they will bring microorganisms unknown to us, which will set off a murderous epidemic among us. We know the elaborate precautions that are taken with our earthly astronauts before and after a trip to the moon, to make sure they have no harmful microbes on them.* It is odd that this problem has been almost totally ignored by those who claim that our planet is now frequented, and has been for a long time, by Martians or other space travelers. Although it is not decisive proof, the fact that we have not suffered any

---

* May it not be that baptism (purification by water, washing) was only the traditional sanitary precaution taught by extraterrestrial Superior Ancestors or angels to ward off sin, that is, contamination by microbes or radiation? If extraterrestrials came to our planet in the past, as I believe they did, they must certainly have instituted the rite of ablution as a precaution against epidemics.

particularly notable epidemics for several centuries is evidence against the optimistic views of many Ufologists.

COLONIZATION IN SPACE

Although I have great sympathy for those who believe that extraterrestrials will come to Earth to bring knowledge, peace and universal love, I know very well that such hopes are illusory. The history of conquest over thousands of years shows that man always colonizes out of self-interest and always "pacifies" in bloodbaths.

Will we go to other planets for the purpose of bringing harmony to their possible inhabitants, and furthering their development? Neither the Americans nor the Russians have such a foolishly altruistic idea, and in any case they already know that they will find no form of superior animal life within our solar system. Earthlings will go to other planets to test and develop their technology and, if possible, to exploit the natural resources they will find there.

It is all but certain that if extraterrestrials come to Earth it will be to colonize us, and they may even exterminate us, not by a deliberate act of genocide, but through circumstances whose results we cannot yet foresee.

WHO LOVES NATURE?

Man has never shown altruistic sentiments when discovering an unknown land. When the conquistadores went to South America they turned it into a vast arena where millions of Mayas and Incas were slaughtered. And all over the world, in Oceania, Asia, Africa, "civilized" man has colonized, evangelized, oppressed and enslaved "underdeveloped" people—all the while claiming to be bringing them progress.

As for our ecological propaganda, it is meant not to protect nature out of disinterested love, but to protect us against the choking fumes of air pollution, the gangrenous growth of billboards and the stench of poisoned rivers and lakes.

We cultivate roses because they are beautiful, harmonious and fragrant, but their feelings mean nothing to us. What matters is our personal happiness in seeing a rose, admiring its harmony and enjoying its fragrance.

Man has never *gratuitously* loved any element of the universe: a grain of sand, the grass in a meadow, the animals that graze there, the birds that fly overhead. He has always colonized nature; he has never given brotherly attention to a desert, a meadow, a sheep or the wind. His only concern has always been the personal advantage he can draw from nature. He loves a desert when it contains petroleum, a meadow when it fattens a sheep, a sheep when he can eat it or take its wool, the wind when he can make it turn a windmill.

Man has never tried to raise the mental level of an animal, except as a means of better using it for his own selfish purposes.

In spite of these pessimistic considerations, we can still hope that extraterrestrials will gratuitously help us to solve our problems, become aware of our responsibilities and bring everlasting peace and joy to our planet. We can hope so, but our own example should caution us against letting our imagination lead us into delusion.

Perhaps we should tell ourselves that if Superior Visitors have a fantastic technology, they probably developed it, as we have done, to the detriment of common sense. A compassionate heart is worth more than the greatest conceivable intelligence.

THE DISTANCE BARRIER

With our present system of rocket propulsion, journeys to other planets in our solar system will take years to complete. Such durations now seem unacceptable, but technology will make great progress in the relatively near future: spacecraft will be given the equivalent of normal earthly gravitation and made large enough to contain gardens, swimming pools and other things that will make life aboard them more pleasant. Astronauts will set out with their families, or attractive companions of the opposite sex, on what may have to be regarded as journeys without an assured return.

But rocket propulsion will eventually have to be abandoned. True interplanetary adventure will not begin until we land on a planet inhabited by highly intelligent beings, and while we are nearly certain that such planets exist, we know that even the nearest ones must be several light-years away from Earth. If science continues along the path it is now following, it cannot hope to send living human beings to such distant destinations. Travel in space must therefore be associated with travel in time, probably by means of new concepts of time, space and presently unknown universes.

The mental constructs of Western man do not permit him to assimilate the essence of a space-time continuum with simultaneity of the past, present and future, except in dreams, when the conscious mind is asleep and interpenetrations, coincidences, overlappings and reversals of order and values occur without disorienting or even surprising the awakened subconscious.

This same state of mind, or rather of understanding, is habitual and innate in several peoples called "savages," and it was particularly strong among the Incas, the Mayas and the nomads of Australia. They all lived a "dream time," which bears marked similarities to the space-time continuum, incomprehensible but apprehensible.

Travel to other inhabited planets will probably take place in a great dream, outside our physical and scientific contingencies. I believe it is reasonable to assume the possibility and even the necessity of such an adventure. It is obviously inscribed in the future program of mankind.

The mysterious call that we feel from the sky, the help that mankind has expected from it for thousands of years, and the steps toward interplanetary travel taken by American and Soviet rockets are signs that other space travelers have already succeeded in reaching Earth and that our memory chromosomes have transmitted a memory of it.

THE AGE OF MIRACLES

In the past sorcerers said they could make an absent person's image appear in a mirror, converse with another initiate thousands of miles away, give an order in one country and be instantly obeyed in another, make an object speak, bring back images of a scene in the past, travel on a flying carpet and go in the astral body to another planet or into another world. Except for ignorant people, no one took these claims seriously. Except for poets, too, and initiates.

Ignorant people, poets and initiates were right, because nearly all those things have been accomplished in our age of miracles. Television transmits images around the world and from the moon to the earth; radio transmits words of all kinds, including orders and prayers; millions of people fly in airplanes every day; phonograph records speak; submarines dive; astronauts speed through space; cinema takes us back in time and resuscitates a queen's coronation or a fishing trip that took place twenty years ago; dead actors come back to life on film.

It is only a question of time until the last of the miracles claimed in the past is actually achieved. I believe that agravity will give us a modern version of the flying carpet within a few years. Travel in the astral body will also be accomplished: people will go to planets hundreds of thousands of light-years away, live and converse there, and come back to Earth.

Not many of us dare to believe in such adventures, more wondrous than those of the Knights of the Round Table. Yet millions of people live in the midst of miracles and take them for granted. The average person refuses to believe in the impossible, and yet he talks on a telephone, travels in an airplane, train or car, uses the vast energy of electricity in his home and watches televised images of events taking place on the other side of the world.

TRAVEL IN THE ASTRAL BODY

Travel in time and space is probably not a problem of hours, seconds and miles, because space-time is an unknown with multiple dimensions of which we have only a faint apperception. We do not even know if it is a concrete reality or a potential postulate belonging to what Buddha called *maya*.

Hypothetically, it is possible to assume that the fantastic journey from Earth to another planetary system in the universe will take place *instantaneously,* just as, by thought, we can instantaneously go to Mars or Sirius.

Are signals or messages being sent to us by extraterrestrials? It is quite possible, even though we do not perceive them, since our present knowledge in telecommunication does not go beyond material waves. Until quite recently man had no way of perceiving radio waves.

But in the twentieth century the image of a man working on the moon comes to us in color, and will soon come to us in relief. Cinema in relief is already on the verge of being accomplished, and holography makes it possible to examine a distant object from the front, back and sides *at the same time*.

It is therefore rational to think that at some time in the future we will have transmitters that can send explorers in relief images to other planetary systems. And of course intelligent beings in other systems will be able to make the same kind of transmissions to Earth.

Image-astronauts will travel to other planets and explore them as if they were there. At first they will not be able to make physical contact with a planet: bathe in its seas, taste its food, smell flowers, touch objects, and so on. But we can trust the science of the future to make it possible for explorers to experience other planetary systems physically, as in a dream.

In a dream the sleeper actually projects himself into a different universe where his senses have the notion of reality (odors, tastes, colors, sounds, etc.), but that reality is only a potentiality to the waking conscious mind. The "potentiality-reality" of dreams gives us a foretaste of the miracle we can expect in the future.

This idea is supported by another consideration: esoteric traditions, along with the philosopher Henri Bergson, maintain that thought is creative; in other words, that thought has a power of mass and materialization, with the presumed waves of thought being transformed into dense matter.

A kind of materialization of an image-astronaut, without actual movement of his physical body, is a real possibility. If it is achieved, travel in the astral body to another planet will be equivalent, as in a dream, to travel in the material body, with certain prerogatives of reality. Initiates are said to have already accomplished such travel, but we have no proof of it.

WHAT HAS BEEN
IS LIKE WHAT WILL BE

Will contact with extraterrestrial civilizations bring us mortal danger or beneficial teachings? Only experience will tell, assuming that contact takes place. And I believe it will, since our scientific élites are already working toward it.

One thing is certain: all earthly human beings, from scientists to plowmen, are haunted by the conquest of the sky, as if they rejected their adherence to the Earth Mother and preferred to seek their origin and home-land outside of our galaxy. Spiritualists and nearly all religious believers have long had a similar attitude: for them, paradise is always in some indefinite ethereal region, beyond our known, everyday world.

Traditionalists are optimistic, probably with good reason. They believe that the First Fathers, or Superior Ancestors, once came from the sky, that Venusians were responsible for the development of ancient civil-izations, that extraterrestrials prompted the giant draw-ings of Nasca and the engravings on Dr. Cabrera's stones, and that they are depicted in the carvings on the Gate of the Sun at Tiahuanaco.

Our dreams and desire-images may be only deceptive figments of our imagination, but distorted resurgences of an earlier life, arising from the subconscious, fore-shadow the fantastic destiny for which we hope, the destiny that has been inscribed in the human program since its origin.

As Hermes Trismegistus said, what is above is like what is below, and what has been is like what will be.